the big book of
candles

the big book of
candles

over 40 step-by-step candlemaking projects

sue heaser

NORTH LIGHT BOOKS

Cincinnati, Ohio

Dedication
To my father, Gordon Lea, who gave me so much.

Distributed to the trade and craft markets in North America by

North Light Books
and imprint of F & W Publications, Inc.
4700 East Galbraith Road
Cincinnati, OH 45236

(800) 289-0963

Originally published in 2002 by
New Holland Publishers (UK) Ltd

ISBN 1-58180-324-9

Senior Editor: Clare Johnson
Editor: Gillian Haslam
Production: Hazel Kirkman
Design: Peter Crump
Photographer: Shona Wood
Editorial Direction: Rosemary Wilkinson

1 3 5 7 9 10 8 6 4 2

Reproduction by Modern Age Repro House Ltd, Hong Kong
Printed and bound by Times Offset (M) Sdn. Bhd., Malaysia

Note
The author and publishers have made every effort to ensure that all
instructions given in this book are safe and accurate, but they cannot accept
liability for any resulting injury or loss or damage to either property or
person, whether direct or consequential and howsoever arising.

Acknowledgements
I would like to thank Inger John, a master candlemaker, who taught me how to
dip beautiful candles. David Coffey showed me how to make his wizard candle
which I adapted for the angel candle in this book. Thanks are also due to
David Constable of Candle Makers Suppliers for kindly lending materials and
equipment for photography.

contents

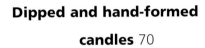

introduction

Candlemaking is a truly delightful hobby. The materials are irresistible: the soft texture of the wax, the vivid dyes, the fragrance of beeswax and candle scents – all are luscious to handle and a treat for the senses. Added to this is the gentle pace of the making – you cannot rush a candle, it will set in good time. This must surely have a calming effect on those of us who never seem to stop in our busy lives.

But it is not only the making of the candles; it is the burning of them as well that makes this ancient craft so pleasing. Candles are temporary decorations – they are made to be lit. A well-made candle will look its best while burning, when the translucent wax glows in the flame to make a whole that is much greater than the sum of its parts. Fragrance is given off, atmosphere created, eyes made to shine, and the candle slowly burns down. Candles grouped in a candelabra at a dinner table, candles twinkling in jars around the edges of a garden, and great pillar candles flickering quietly in a cathedral: what a joy they all are!

Candles are as popular today as they have ever been and perhaps this is because we want relief from our high-tech lives. When I was a child, we lived in a remote area that used to have regular power failures. On these occasions the candles would be brought out and lit and tea was consumed by magical candlelight. Those were the best times of all, when familiar faces looked soft and different, the room took on a color unseen in normal life, and shadows would appear that were never usually there. Bedtime stories seemed more special on those candlelit nights.

This book is all about how to make candles. If you have never attempted candlemaking, you will find everything here to help you start. If you are already accomplished, I hope you will find new inspirations and new ideas. But please, whatever you do, remember that those candles are for burning. So light your candles and enjoy them; don't let them just sit decoratively on the shelf gathering dust. And once they are burned, you have a wonderful excuse to make some more.

Sue Heaser –

materials and equipment

This chapter covers all the main materials that you will need to make your own candles. Candlemaking has very simple requirements for equipment and you will probably have most things that you need already in your home. To begin with, you only need some paraffin wax, a wick and an improvised mold to produce simple candles that will delight you. However, you will soon discover that just a few extra materials will make your candlemaking much more fun and will help you to produce candles to be proud of. All the materials listed here are readily available from craft materials retailers or specialist candlemaker suppliers. If you have difficulty finding any of these, see pages 142–143 for mail order suppliers.

wax

Paraffin Wax
This is the most popular wax for making candles and is widely available from art and craft outlets and specialist candlemaker suppliers. It comes either as large slabs of wax, which need breaking up before use, or in the form of pellets which are much easier to weigh and melt.

Paraffin wax is available with various melting points, but the standard all-purpose wax that you find in your local craft store usually has a melting point of around 133–140°F (56–60°C) and this is ideal for the projects in this book. Paraffin wax is normally sold uncolored and, when melted, looks just like water. It burns with virtually no smell and you can

microcrystalline soft

microcrystalline hard

Vybar

gel wax

paraffin pellets

beeswax

dip-and-carve wax

stearin

candle sand

color it with dyes, add scents, alter its translucency, and add various other waxes to make it soft and malleable or hard and long burning. You can pour it, mold it, carve it, chop it up, make sheets out of it, drizzle it and generally thoroughly enjoy handling it! It is also non-toxic and safe to use in your kitchen if you follow simple safety guidelines (see page 16).

Dip-and-Carve Wax

This is a proprietary blended wax that is sold for making carved candles. When partly cool, it is less prone to cracking than ordinary paraffin wax. I use it for pouring wax sheets that are going to be rolled or hand-molded while soft.

Modeling Wax

This is available already colored in tubs or blocks. You immerse the wax in hot water until it becomes malleable and then use it to make hand-formed candles. However, the resulting candles are very soft and usually burn rapidly. You can make your own modeling wax by melting together 2½oz (70g) microcrystalline soft with 1oz (30g) paraffin wax, a teaspoon of petroleum jelly and wax dye.

Beeswax

Pure beeswax, while relatively costly, makes glorious candles. It is slow burning and has a wonderful golden color and a heavenly fragrance. Just handling beeswax softens my hands and makes me think of summer! It is much stickier than paraffin wax, so if you use it to make molded candles, you will need to brush the mold with mold release or vegetable oil. I find beeswax is best added to paraffin wax because this makes it easier to mold. You can add as little as 10 percent beeswax to get the benefits, but a mixture of half beeswax to half paraffin wax plus 10 percent stearin makes beautiful golden candles.

Beeswax is also sold in sheets that have a honeycomb pattern and can be used to make simple rolled candles (see page 37).

The sheets come in natural beeswax color as well as many other shades.

Candle Sand

This is also called powdered wax and comes already colored. You simply pour the candle sand into a suitable container, insert a wick and light it for an instant candle. The sand will float on water so you can make unusual water candles by floating a layer of sand, complete with its wick, on top of a glass of water.

Gel Wax

This is an exciting way to make candles. Gel wax sets to a rubbery solid that is as clear as water. It is used to make striking container candles, particularly in glass containers, which show it off.

Gel wax is not really a wax at all but a mixture of oil and a polymer. It melts at 194–212°F (90–100°C) so it is best to melt it over a direct heat source. Like cooking oil, it can catch fire if overheated so watch the pan at all times. Gel wax candles burn with a smaller flame than ordinary paraffin wax candles. The wick should be trimmed shorter, to about ¼in (6mm).

You can use all kinds of objects as inclusions in gel wax. Non-flammable objects are the safest to use, and include shells, beads, glass nuggets and charms. You can also color the gel with powdered dyes, but not with ordinary wax dye discs.

Microcrystalline Wax

This wax comes in two types, hard and soft. They are both useful for mixing with paraffin wax to change the consistency depending on what type of candle you are making:

Microcrystalline Hard This is added to paraffin wax in a tiny proportion – just one percent or 1 teaspoon to 1lb (500g) of paraffin wax. It makes the wax stronger and slower burning because it raises the melting point. Add it to dipped candles, hurricane shells and any other candle

where strength is important. If it is added to wax pieces when making chunk candles, the chunks are less likely to melt when the mold is filled with melted wax.

Microcrystalline Soft This wax has a low melting point and is added to paraffin wax to make it soft and malleable. It is useful when making container candles because it makes the wax stick to the containers better. Add 10 percent or 1 tablespoon per 3½oz (100g). You can also use it to make your own modeling wax (see above).

wax additives

Stearin

Stearin is a white crystalline substance usually made from palm oil. It comes in a powder form and is a useful additive to paraffin wax in order to achieve certain effects. It helps the candle to burn longer; it intensifies wax dyes; it makes the wax more opaque; and it makes the wax shrink on cooling so that the candle is easier to remove from its mold.

Stearin should not be used in latex molds because it will rot them; use Vybar instead (see below). Stearin should not be used if you want your candle to be as translucent as possible, such as candles containing inclusions. Container candles should not contain stearin because it will make the wax shrink away from the sides of the container.

The usual amount to use is 10 percent of the weight of the paraffin wax, or one level tablespoon per 3½oz (100g) of wax. Quantities are not really critical so there is no need to measure to a fine degree of accuracy.

Vybar

This is a proprietary additive that has similar effects as stearin but is used with latex molds. Add one percent of the weight of the wax used, or approximately ½ teaspoon per 3½oz (100g) wax.

wicks

The wick is really the most important part of the candle. The wax is the fuel for the flame but the wick is the means by which it burns. Wicks are designed to curve over at the top when burning so that the tip is constantly being burnt away and does not need trimming as the candle burns down.

It is important to choose the correct wick for the type and size of candle. The candle will not burn successfully if the wrong wick is used. Wicks come in different sizes according to the width of the candle. For example, a 1in (25mm) wick should be used for a 1in (25mm) diameter candle; a 1½in (38mm) wick should be used for a 1½in (38mm) diameter candle and so on. If in doubt, use a wick that is too small. An oversized wick will cause the candle to smoke. Small wicks can be used

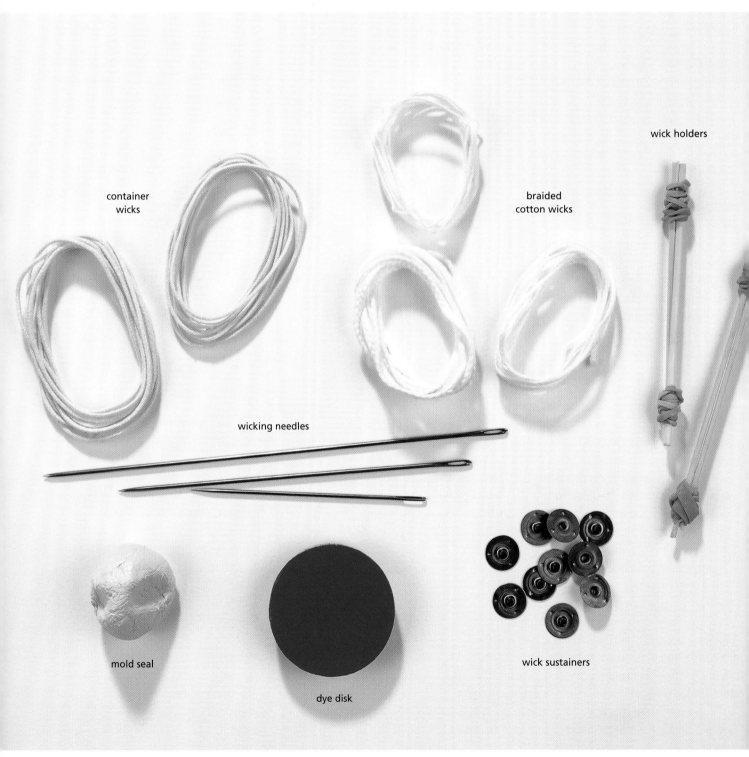

container wicks

braided cotton wicks

wick holders

wicking needles

mold seal

dye disk

wick sustainers

to make the candle burn down in a cavity to keep the flame away from decorated sides. Large wicks tend to burn with a much larger flame than smaller wicks because they draw more molten wax up them to be burned.

If you are making a candle of variable thickness, such as a pyramid, you will have to compromise and accept that some parts of the candle will burn better than others. In this instance, use a wick that is the right size for the middle section of the candle.

There are many different sizes and types of wick but choosing the right one for a candle is not difficult. All wicks should be primed before use by soaking in hot wax (see page 18).

Braided Cotton Wicks

These are the most widely available and are used for most kinds of dipped, molded and hand-formed candles. They are available in sizes ranging from ¼in (6mm) up to 4in (100mm) and more. You can usually buy wick by the meter (yard) or in large rolls of about 33 yards (30m) so you can then cut off the length of wick that you need for a project.

Container Wicks

The wax in container candles may liquefy if it gets hot enough so these wicks have a core of either paper or metal that will hold the wick vertically at all times. Container wicks come in different sizes, just like braided cotton wicks, and you need to choose the wick to suit the diameter of the container (see above).

wax dye

Wax dye comes in various forms. These are the most common.

Dye Disks or Squares

These are the easiest kind of dyes for beginners to use. They contain pigment, stearin and a small amount of wax, and are normally labeled with the amount of wax that they will color to full strength. You then need to work out the quantity of dye that you need for any given quantity of wax. (See page 17 for full details of coloring candles.) Candles colored with dye discs can fade or bleed in time because the color is not as stable as powder dye.

Powder Dyes

These pigments are extremely strong and only the tiniest quantities are needed for a single candle. They are more colorfast than dye disks but harder to use because of the tiny amounts needed.

other candlemaking materials

Wax Scents

Scenting candles adds a whole new dimension to the art of candlemaking. Not only can you design the shape and color of your candles, you can also add fragrance to scent the room when the candles burn. Proprietary candle scents are available from candlemaking suppliers and these can be guaranteed to burn safely. However, many essential oils work beautifully in candles and while they are quite costly, they are concentrated natural substances and have the best fragrances of all. (See page 19 for how to scent candles.)

Wick Sustainers

Wick sustainers are used to anchor a wick in the center of a container while you fill it with wax. They are small metal disks with a central tube into which you push the end of a wick. The tube is then crimped onto the wick with pliers. Sustainers are also useful for holding the wick in an improvised mold which does not have a wick hole in the bottom. (See page 18 for how to attach a wick sustainer.)

Wicking Needles

These large needles come in several sizes up to about 6in (15cm) long and are used to thread the wick through the end of a latex mold. You can use a large darning needle instead.

Wick Holder

This is a wonderful piece of equipment that is used to keep the wick centrally positioned in a mold or container while the wax sets. You can make this easily using a bamboo skewer and two elastic bands (see page 19).

Mold Seal

This is a tacky kind of putty that is used to seal around the wick where it protrudes from the wick hole at the bottom of a mold. You can use putty adhesive instead.

Mold Release

This is a thin liquid that can be painted onto the inside of flexible molds to aid release. A thin coat of vegetable oil can be used instead.

Wax Glue

A very sticky form of wax that has many uses such as for attaching wax decorations to candles or for securing the base of a wick sustainer in the bottom of a container.

Latex

This is a wonderful material for making your own flexible molds. You can use air-drying clay to sculpt a simple shape as a master for a candle and then paint on layers of latex. The mold is peeled off the master when it is dry and can be used to mold your own, individual candles (see page 66). Latex is available from candlemaking suppliers and sculpting suppliers.

candle decorating materials

Appliqué Wax
These thin, flexible sheets of wax come in a range of colors and are used to decorate candles with shapes and motifs. They can be cut with scissors or small cutters and come with a paper backing which you peel off before applying the shape to the candle. Appliqué wax will stick more firmly if you press each piece onto the candle with your hand for a short time to warm it.

Candle Lacquer
There are various proprietary varnishes and lacquers available for painting on to candles to give them a shine or to protect added decorations such as gold leaf. Do not use ordinary varnish because it is not intended to be burnt.

Paints
Acrylic paints work well on candles but you need to prime the surface first or the paint will not stick. Simply rub a thin coat of acrylic paint, of the same color as the candle, over the candle surface and allow it to dry before painting.

Gold Leaf
Real gold leaf costs a small fortune but the artificial kind is just as good for candlemaking purposes. Buy the loose leaf which comes in various metallic and variegated colors as well as gold, silver and copper. Leaf flakes are used in several projects and they are simply flakes of colored leaf.

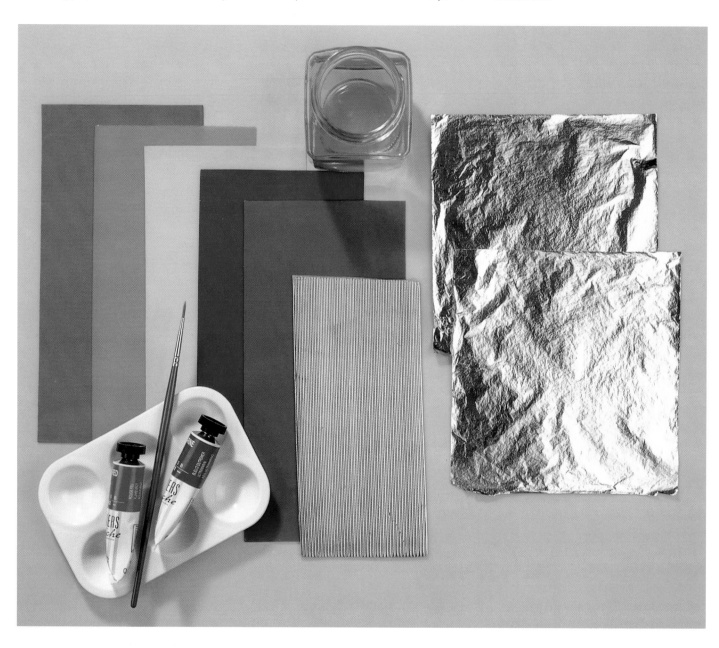

general equipment

Wax Melting Pan
An old saucepan with a good lip for pouring is ideal for melting wax. It is often recommended that you should melt wax in a double boiler so that you do not accidentally let the wax overheat and burn. Provided you are careful and never leave the pan unattended, you will find an ordinary saucepan far quicker to use. I like to melt small quantities of wax in a metal jug so that the wax can be poured out easily without the problems of decanting.

Thermometer
You will need a thermometer to measure the temperature of the wax and an ordinary cooking or sugar thermometer is perfect for candles. It should be able to measure temperatures between at least 120°F and 250°F (50°C and 120°C). A thermometer with a brass back is more expensive than a simple glass tube thermometer, but more durable.

Dipping Can
This is used for overdipping molded candles as well as for making dipped tapers. Proprietary dipping cans are available from candlemaker suppliers but they can be quite expensive – you can easily improvise with any tall metal can that can be placed on a direct heat source and that is watertight. A large pet food can will suffice if you only want to dip small candles but if you want to make long tapers, you will need a can at least 1in (2.5cm) taller than the height of the candles you want to make.

Pouring Pitcher

A pitcher with a good lip is very useful for pouring hot wax into molds and topping up molded candles. A metal pitcher can be used to heat the wax as well.

Ladle

Useful for ladling hot wax from a saucepan into a small pitcher for pouring.

Scales

You will need a basic set of kitchen scales for weighing wax. These only need an accuracy of about 1oz (25g). All the quantities smaller than this are given in tablespoon and teaspoon measures in the projects.

Skewers

Bamboo skewers are invaluable for stirring dyes into wax and piercing candles before topping off.

Smooth-surfaced Board

This is used for pouring sheets of wax to make rolled or hand-formed candles. An ordinary chopping board with a smooth melamine surface is ideal.

Water Bath

Water baths are often used to speed up the cooling of molded candles. Use any large bowl or plastic ice cream container that is large enough to hold the mold. You will also need some kind of weight to place on top of a rigid mold to stop it floating. A jam jar full of water or a large pebble both work well.

Newspaper and Waxed Paper

Spilt wax is difficult to remove so it is best to cover your kitchen surfaces with several layers of newspaper before starting. Wax does not stick to greaseproof paper so keep a sheet handy for laying waxy implements on.

Containers for Leftover Wax

The type of heatproof container that is used to package chilled meals is ideal for pouring remnants of wax into. When the wax has cooled, you can just pop it out of the container and store it for future use.

Craft Knife

Use a craft knife to cut and score lines in card when making molds. It can also be used to cut soft wax.

Cutting Mat

A cutting mat will protect your working surface whenever you use a craft knife and it can be used again and again. Alternatively, you could try working on a few layers of corrugated cardboard.

Scissors

Use scissors to trim the wicks of finished candles and to cut out paper templates.

Masking Tape

Use masking tape to mark measurements on molds, to tape down templates or stencils and to paint straight lines.

Ruler

An ordinary stationery ruler is used to measure depths on a mold. You will also need to draw straight lines against a ruler when making your own molds. Use a craft knife against a metal ruler to score or cut straight lines.

Paper Towel

Paper towel is indispensable for mopping up wax and cleaning equipment.

Pliers

Pliers are useful for securing wicks in a wick sustainers as well as pulling a wick through a hole in a mold.

molds

Molded candles are relatively easy to make and there is a good range of proprietary molds to choose from. The following are the most commonly used.

Rigid Molds

Rigid molds are used to make candles in bold geometric shapes such as cubes, cylinders and pyramids. They can be made from glass, metal or plastic. Plastic molds are usually the cheapest but take care not to damage the inside of the mold. If stacking several molds, place a piece of paper inside to prevent scratching. Do not use rigid plastic molds with candle scents or fill them with wax heated to over 175°F (80°C) or they may be damaged.

Latex Molds

Widely available in a wonderful range of shapes and sizes, latex molds are inexpensive and easy to use. The stretchable quality of the latex means that these molds can be made in more elaborate shapes such as animals, fruit and flowers.

Improvised Molds

There is no need to use purchased molds at all if you do not want to, because you can make your own out of everyday objects and recycled containers. Any container such as a yogurt container, drinking glass or cake tin can be used provided it does not have any overhangs that would prevent you removing the finished candle (see page 31). You can also make molds out of stiff cardboard (see page 60).

Latex Mold Support

These wire frames are sold to hold up a latex mold while the wax cools. You can make your own by cutting a hole in a piece of stiff card that is large enough for the mold to fit into so that it hangs by its flange. The card support is then set onto the rim of a vase or pitcher with the mold hanging inside.

getting started

This chapter tells you everything you need to know to start making your own candles. Candlemaking is not a difficult craft to learn and in many ways, it is similar to cooking: you need to use the right ingredients and follow the 'recipes' accurately. The basic techniques are simple to learn and once you have mastered them, you will soon enjoy experimenting and creating your own candle designs.

the work area

A kitchen is an ideal place to make candles because it contains the basic requirement of a burner to heat the wax, a supply of water, and work surfaces. Lay plenty of sheets of newspaper on the floor and over the work surfaces to catch any spilt wax and make cleaning up easier. Wax dropped onto a tiled floor can make it very slippery, even after cleaning up. Keep a roll of paper towel handy for spills and mopping the bottom of pitchers or pans if they drip.

Gather together everything you need before you start so you are not tempted to leave wax heating unattended while you fetch something. I never leave the kitchen with the burner turned on.

safety guidelines

Candlemaking is a safe hobby provided that you keep to a few simple guidelines.

• Wax has a low melting point and if it gets too hot, it can burst into flames just like cooking oil. Treat it with respect and never leave a pan unattended.
• If wax catches fire, smother the flames with a wet towel or kitchen fire blanket. Do NOT attempt to quench the flames with water because this will splash burning wax everywhere.
• Always use a thermometer when heating wax so that you know that it is not getting too hot.
• If you spill hot wax on your skin, immediately hold it under the cold tap. Hot wax rarely scalds if you keep it to the temperatures required for normal candlemaking.
• Use oven mitts when handling hot cans of wax that do not have handles.
• Keep pets and young children out of the kitchen while you are making candles.
• Set improvised molds in a container while pouring to catch any leaking wax.

how much wax to use

If you are using a new or improvised mold, you can estimate the weight of wax needed by filling the mold with water and then pouring it out into a measuring jug. For every 3½fl oz (100ml) of water, you will need 3½oz (100g) of wax. This is a generous estimate to ensure that you do not melt too little wax.

melting wax

Using scales, weigh out the quantity of wax required. Pellet wax is easy to melt, but if the wax is in slab form, break it into smaller pieces with a screwdriver and hammer, holding the screwdriver as a chisel and banging the end of its handle with a hammer. Make sure you do this on a surface that cannot be damaged (an old chopping board works well).

Place the wax in a saucepan and heat it on the burner using a medium heat at first, then turn it down to a gentle heat when the wax begins to melt. Once you start heating the wax, do not leave it

melting wax

testing the temperature

unattended at any time. Place a thermometer in the wax and heat until almost all the wax has melted. Turn off the heat and the heat of the pan will melt the remaining wax. Never allow the wax temperature to go higher than 212°F (100°C) except in special projects such as the Sand Candle (see page 80).

You can also heat the wax in a double boiler or in a can placed on a trivet in a large saucepan of boiling water. This takes quite a long time, but at least if you do forget the heating wax, it is unlikely to cause a fire. When heating wax in this way, do not overfill the saucepan of water or the wax container may float and tip up. Take care that the pan does not boil dry.

Once the wax is at the correct temperature, you can pour it directly from the saucepan or ladle it into a pitcher for pouring into a mold. I like to heat wax in a metal pitcher that can be placed directly on the heat source because this avoids having to decant hot wax for pouring. If you decant wax, warm the pitcher first to prevent the temperature of the wax dropping too much too quickly.

If you are using stearin, microcrystalline soft or Vybar, they can be melted with the wax. Additives with a higher melting point, such as microcrystalline hard or pearly white dye, should be melted first with a small amount of wax, to ensure that they melt thoroughly before you add the remainder of the wax.

Always wait 24 hours before lighting a newly made candle. Otherwise, the wax will not be completely cool and the candle will burn away too quickly.

coloring wax

Coloring candles is great fun and everything you learnt at school about blue and yellow making green comes to life when you work with the dyes. The easiest dyes to use are dye disks or rectangular cakes. These have the quantity of wax that they will dye to full color marked on the pack. Powder colors are harder to use because they are so strong.

How Much Dye to Use

When you open a new dye disk or block, score it into eight equal sections with a knife. If the block dyes 4½lb (2kg) of wax, each section will dye 9oz (250g). Cut off sections as you need them – the remaining score lines mean that you will always know how much to use, even when the block is half used.

If you are using powder colors, you will only need enough powder to cover the tip of a knife to color 3½oz (100g) wax.

Mixing Colors

Try combining different colors of wax dye to get a greater variety of colors. A small amount of black dye added to most colors will give subtle shades (apart from yellow which looks awful!).

Pastel Colors

You will need only a tiny amount of dye to make pastels. Use about one-eighth of the normal amount, or less. It is easier to add more dye if the color is too pale. If the color is too dark, pour out about half the wax in the pan, add an equal quantity of plain wax and melt again. You can use the unused wax in another project. Pearly white dye is useful for making lovely pastels.

Melting Dye

Melt the dye with a little wax first, then add the rest of the wax and continue melting. If you are using stearin, melt the dye in this before adding the wax.

Testing the Color

The color of the molten wax in the pan gives little indication of the color of the set wax. To check the color, pour a teaspoonful of wax onto a sheet of greaseproof paper. It will set in a few moments to show what the actual finished color will be.

cutting a block of dye

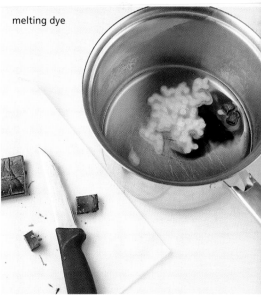

melting dye

testing the color

preparing the wick

Choose the size and type of wick that is correct for the candle (see page 10). Wicks for all candles should be primed, or soaked in wax, before use so that they burn well and cannot absorb any water during the molding process. Drop the length of wick into melted wax and leave it to soak for about five seconds. Scoop it out with a skewer and hold it above the pan until it stops dripping and cools a little. Pull the wick straight and lay it onto a sheet of waxed paper to harden.

It is a good idea to prime a selection of long lengths of wick in uncolored wax so that you have a ready supply that can be cut to size as needed.

Using a Wick Sustainer

Use these to anchor the wick in the center of a container or improvised mold. Push the

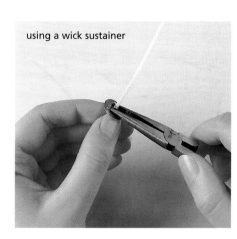
using a wick sustainer

priming the wick

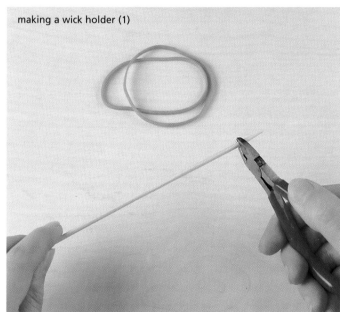
making a wick holder (1)

straightening a primed wick

making a wick holder (2)

primed wick into the small tube at the top of the sustainer and nip the metal with pliers to hold the wick firmly. Use a dab of wax glue to secure the sustainer to the bottom of a container or mold.

Making a Wick Holder

A wick holder is essential for keeping the wick centrally positioned. This one is incredibly simple to make. Cut the sharp point off a bamboo barbecue skewer and then cut the skewer in half. Place the two halves together and wrap each end with a small rubber band. You can now use the holder to clip the wick in place in the center of the mold by pulling the two halves apart and trapping the wick between them. The wick holder simply rests on the top of the mold.

scenting wax

Candle scents are very concentrated and should have the amount of wax that they will scent marked on them. Quantities given vary with the manufacturers but I usually find about 1 teaspoon will scent 7oz (200g) wax. Candle scents have been tested on wax and are known to work well; do not be tempted to use ordinary perfume to scent candles.

Many essential oils can be used to scent candles but you should test them first (see below). I find that 5 drops per 3½oz (100g) of wax is a good guide, although this will vary with different oils. Citronella, pine and rose geranium all smell delicious when used in candles.

Before using an essential oil in a candle, test that it will not produce an unpleasant smell when it is burnt by dipping a primed wick into the oil and lighting it. Blow the flame out and then sniff.

Stir the scent or oil into the melted wax just before you pour it into the mold. Too much heat will spoil or vaporize the fragrance. Do not use scents in rigid plastic molds which may be damaged.

flattening the candle base

If the bottom of the candle made in a mold is uneven, cover the base of a small pan with a sheet of foil and heat the pan gently. Hold the bottom of the candle onto the foil for a few seconds to melt the wax and neaten the base. The foil prevents the pan from being coated in wax.

recycling leftover wax

One of the bonuses of making candles is that there is very little waste. Wax can be melted down and used again, and you can even use up the leftover ends of candles that have been burnt.

If you let wax cool and solidify in your saucepan or pitcher, you can simply heat it up again to use or to pour out. Leftover wax can be poured into plastic food containers, left to harden and then removed and stored.

If recycled wax is dirty, lay a piece of paper towel inside a sieve and pour the melted wax through this into a container.

cleaning your equipment

After pouring waste wax into containers for storage, immediately wipe around the saucepan or pitcher while it is still warm with a paper towel. If the utensil is used only for wax, it needs no further cleaning. To clean a saucepan thoroughly for food use, first wipe out as above, then scour in hot soapy water or wash in the dishwasher. Do not put saucepans covered with a lot of wax in the dishwasher or the wax may clog the drains when it sets.

Molds should be cleaned thoroughly of any traces of wax after use or the next candle made in the mold will be hard to remove. Plastic molds are easy to scratch so take care when cleaning them. If a lot of wax is stuck to the inside of the mold, immerse in 175°F (80°C) soapy water and most of the wax will float off. Finally, clean inside the mold with a rag dipped in methylated spirits (denatured alcohol).

Clean latex molds by turning them inside out and peeling off any wax, then immerse in hot soapy water to clean them.

General Cleaning Up

This is easy to do if you have laid sheets of newspaper over your floor and work surfaces. Here are more tips to make cleaning up simple.

• Never pour molten wax down the sink as it will set in the waste pipes.
• If you get melted wax on your clothes, scrape off as much as possible, then cover the spot with a paper towel and iron with a hot iron to absorb the wax into the paper. Finally, give the fabric a hot wash.
• Wax spilt on a carpet should be rubbed with an ice cube, then scraped off and ironed as above.
• Remove wax from wooden surfaces by gently scraping. Wax can be removed from metal surfaces by pouring boiling water over the wax.

projects

Chinese bowl

Container candles are some of the easiest to make because they do not need a mold. You can have fun choosing a wax color to complement the container and here, a pretty blue picks out the Chinese-style patterning on the bowl.

you will need

- Paper or metal core wick for a 2½in (6cm) wide candle, 2½in (6cm) long, primed
- Wick sustainer
- Wax glue
- A pretty china bowl, about 4in (10cm) diameter and 2in (5cm) deep
- Pliers
- Wick holder
- 5oz (150g) paraffin wax
- 1 tbsp (15g) microcrystalline soft
- Blue wax dye
- Wax melting pan or metal pitcher
- Thermometer
- Skewer

 **timing** 30 minutes plus setting time

tip The wax in container candles can liquefy during burning so use a paper or metal core wick that will not collapse.

variation Try adding 5 drops of lavender essential oil to the wax just before pouring it into the bowl.

1 Attach the wick to the wick sustainer (see page 18). Smear a little wax glue onto the base of the sustainer and press it onto the bottom of the bowl. Clip the top of the wick in place with the wick holder, ensuring it is in the center of the bowl.

2 Melt the wax and the microcrystalline soft together with the blue dye. When the temperature reaches 175°F (80°C), pour the wax into the bowl to a depth of about ½in (15mm) below the rim. If your bowl has a design around the inner top edge, fill it to an appropriate point to set this off.

3 Leave the wax to cool until the surface has set and the center has sunk. Pierce down with a skewer around the wick into the molten wax below. Reheat the blue wax to 175°F (80°C) and top the candle up, filling until the added wax just reaches the sides of the bowl.

4 Leave the wax to cool again and top up once more if necessary. There is no need to worry about the hot wax running down between the set wax and the sides of the bowl because this will not be visible with a china bowl.

5 When the candle is completely cool, remove the wick holder and trim the wick to ½in (13mm).

champagne gel candle

Gel wax is used in this project to suggest bubbling champagne, and flecks of artificial gold leaf add to the sparkle. These candles make a splendid display for a celebration table setting.

you will need

- Paper or metal core wick for a 2in (50mm) candle, the depth of the glass plus 1in (25mm), primed in hot gel wax
- Wick sustainer
- Pliers
- Wineglass
- Wax glue

- Wick holder
- 3½oz (100g) candle gel wax
- Wax melting pan or metal pitcher
- Skewer
- Artificial metallic leaf flakes, or sheets in a mixture of colors, torn into small pieces

timing 30 minutes plus setting time

tip Gel wax has to be heated to a higher temperature than paraffin wax for it to melt. It will also set noticeably faster with no need for topping off.

1 Push one end of the wick into the wick sustainer and squeeze the hole shut with pliers to hold the wick firmly. Stand the wick in the glass, using a smear of wax glue to hold down the wick sustainer. Clip the wick holder around the wick to hold it in the center of the glass. Heat the glass in a warm oven (175°F/80°C/ gas mark ⅛) for 15 minutes.

2 Melt the gel in a saucepan or metal pitcher over a very gentle heat. Pour some melted gel into the glass to a depth of about ⅜in (1cm). Give the gel a gentle stir with a skewer to incorporate a few bubbles for a champagne effect.

3 Leave the layer of gel to cool for 10 minutes until it has set. Place a scatter of metal leaf flakes all over the surface of the gel and arrange them with the tip of a skewer. Now pour in another ⅜in (1cm) layer of gel, stir gently as before and leave to set. The leaf flakes will be suspended between the two layers.

4 Repeat with two more layers of leaf, covering each with ⅜in (1cm) of gel. Building up layers like this prevents the leaf sinking to the bottom and distributes it evenly throughout the gel. The top of the last layer of gel should be about ⅜in (1cm) from the top of the glass.

5 When the gel is completely cool, remove the wick holder and trim the wick to ¼in (6mm) from the surface. When the wick is lit, the flame will shine down through the gel and light up the leaf.

etched glass globe

Delicate etched glass designs decorate this pretty container candle. Areas of a glass globe are masked with paper shapes and then the whole is sprayed with a proprietary glass spray to give the effect of etching without the need for acids. Always remember to warm glass containers before pouring in hot wax. Otherwise, they may crack.

you will need

- A glass globe, about 3in (7.5cm) diameter
- Denatured alcohol
- Cloth
- Stick-on star labels
- Newspaper
- Sheet of scrap paper
- Glass etch spray
- Paper or metal core wick for a 2½in (6cm) wide candle, 2½in (6cm) long
- Wick sustainer
- Pliers
- Wax glue
- Wick holder
- 3½oz (100g) paraffin wax
- 1 tbsp (10g) microcrystalline soft
- Red wax dye
- Wax melting pan or metal pitcher
- Thermometer
- Skewer

timing 1 hour plus setting time

tip Glass etch spray is available from craft materials suppliers. You could use a frosted effect glass paint instead.

1 Wipe over the glass globe with methylated spirits to clean it thoroughly and remove any grease. Peel the stars from their backing and press them lightly onto the globe in a regular pattern. Do not press them on too hard or they will be difficult to remove later.

2 Stand the globe on a piece of newspaper or scrap paper. Roll a sheet of paper into a tube and stand it inside the globe to protect the inside from the spray. Following the manufacturers' instructions, spray the glass etch onto the globe with a light waving motion. It is best to build up the etched effect with several light coats. Otherwise, the spray can run.

3 Leave the globe to dry for about 10 minutes. Peel off the stars, taking care not to damage the sprayed surface. Do not leave the stars on for any longer than this or they will become very hard to remove.

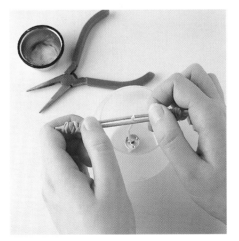

4 Prime the wick and fix it to the wick sustainer. Stand it upright in the center of the globe, using a little wax glue to secure it. Clip the wick in place with the wick holder. Place the globe in a warm oven (200°F/90°C/gas mark ⅛) for 10 minutes to warm it so that it does not crack when you pour in hot wax.

5 Melt the wax with the microcrystalline soft and add enough red dye to give a soft pink (see page 17). Follow the instructions for the Chinese Bowl on page 23 (steps 2–5) to half-fill the globe with wax for a delicate container candle.

crimson column

Rigid molds produce classic candles in bold geometric shapes. Once you have mastered the simple technique, you can enjoy producing candles in a rich variety of colors and shapes. Candles in rigid molds are usually made upside-down, as shown here. This means the bottom of the mold will become the top of the candle while the set surface of the wax will be the base.

you will need

- Rigid mold for a round pillar candle, 4in (10cm) tall and 2½in (6cm) diameter
- Wick for a 2½in (6cm) diameter candle, 6in (15cm) long, primed
- Mold seal
- Wick holder
- 2 tbsp (20g) stearin
- Red dye
- Wax melting pan or metal pitcher
- 7oz (200g) paraffin wax
- Thermometer
- Container (for holding mold)
- Water bath (optional)
- Skewer

timing 30 minutes plus setting time. The candle will set much faster if a water bath is used.

tip Do not overfill when topping off a candle or wax may run down between the mold and the newly set sides of the candle and spoil the candle surface.

1 Thread one end of the primed wick through the hole in the bottom of the mold and seal around it thoroughly with mold seal.

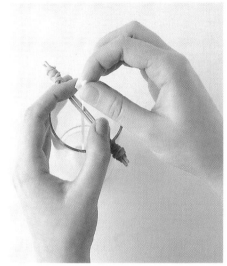

2 Clip the other end of the wick in the wick holder and pull the holder down onto the rim of the mold so that the wick is held straight and tight in the center of the mold.

3 Melt the stearin with the dye and then add the wax. Continue heating until the wax reaches 175°F (80°C). Stand the mold in a container in case the seal leaks, and pour the wax into the mold until it is ½in (13mm) from the rim. Tap the outside of the mold to release any air bubbles and set the mold aside to cool.

4 If you wish, at this point put the mold in a water bath to speed up the cooling and to give your candle a shiny surface. Make sure that the water comes up to the same level as the wax inside the mold or the surface of the candle will show a line. Weight the mold down to prevent it floating.

continued ▶

5 After about 10 minutes in the water bath, or 30–40 minutes, depending on the room temperature, the wax surface will have set into a skin about ⅛in (3mm) thick and the center of the candle will have sunk. Pierce several holes with a skewer around the wick into the molten center of the candle and top off with more wax at 175°F (80°C).

6 Leave the mold to cool until the surface has sunk again and pierce around the wick and top up as before. A large candle may need a further topping off. Now leave the candle to set fully for several hours or overnight.

Troubleshooting for Molded Candles

White horizontal lines on the outside of candle = wax was too cool when poured

Plastic mold damaged or cloudy inside = wax was poured too hot or candle scents were used

Candle will not come out of mold = no stearin was used; wax was poured too cool; no mold release or oil was used; candle mold was not cleaned before use; candle is not completely cold.
Solution: Leave the mold overnight. If the candle is still stuck to the mold, place it in the freezer for about 15 minutes. It should then slide out easily. The last resort is to put the mold in the oven at 160°F/70°C/gas mark ⅛ and leave it until the wax melts. Then clean the mold thoroughly and start again.

Candle burns lop-sidedly = wick was not in the center of the mold

Cracks in the candle = water bath was too cold; topping off wax was too hot

Tiny holes over the surface of the candle = wax was too hot when poured

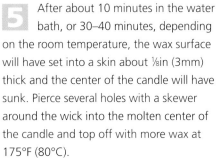

7 When the candle is completely cool, remove the mold seal from around the wick and take off the wick holder. The candle should slide out of the mold when you pull gently on the wick. See the troubleshooting notes if you have difficulty removing a candle from its mold.

8 Cut off the excess wick at the base of the candle, level with the surface of the wax. Flatten the bottom of the candle if necessary (see page 19). Trim back the wick at the top of the candle to about ½in (13mm).

make your own molds

Purchased molds are fun to use and mean that you can make candles in many exciting shapes,

but they are by no means essential for successful candlemaking. Virtually any watertight container

can be used as a mold provided that it does not have overhanging parts that would prevent you

removing the finished candle. Cake tins, cardboard boxes of all shapes, yogurt containers, drinking

glasses – the list is endless. This project shows the principles that can be adapted to many different

improvised molds.

continued ▶

you will need

- Plastic dessert cup
- Vegetable oil and brush
- Wick for a 2½in (6cm) candle, primed, and long enough to reach from the base of the dessert pot to 1in (2.5cm) above the rim
- Wick sustainer
- Pliers
- Wax glue
- Wick holder
- 3½oz (100g) paraffin wax (or sufficient for mold – see page 16)
- 1 tbsp (10g) stearin
- Yellow wax dye
- Wax melting pan or metal pitcher
- Thermometer

Cardboard box:
- Cardboard box
- Sticky tape
- Skewer

timing 30 minutes plus setting time

tip It is often difficult, or impossible, to make a hole for the wick in the base of an improvised mold so this technique uses a wick sustainer instead.

plastic dessert cup mold

1 First test that the plastic cup is able to withstand the temperature of the hot wax. Stand the cup in a bowl or sink, heat some water to 175°F (80°C) and pour it into the cup. Leave the cup to cool for 10 minutes and then check that there is no sign of distortion. Dry the cup thoroughly before using as a mold.

2 Brush over the inside of the cup with vegetable oil. Fix the wick into the wick sustainer. Use a dab of wax glue to stick the bottom of the wick sustainer to the center bottom of the container. Clip the top of the wick in place with the wick holder, ensuring it is centered.

3 Melt the wax and stearin with the dye and heat until it reaches 175°F (80°C). Pour the wax into the mold and leave to set. Pierce and top off with more hot wax as usual.

4 When you top off for the last time, pour only enough wax to make a central pool around the wick because the top surface becomes the top of the candle when using improvised molds. This will then set to make a smooth top to the candle.

5 When the candle has set, you should be able to flex the sides of the cup to free the candle from the mold. Slide the candle out of the cup and trim the wick to ⅜in (10mm).

using a cardboard box

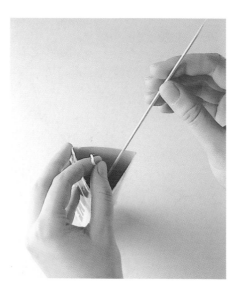

1 Tape over the seams of the box firmly with sticky tape. This will prevent the box falling apart if the hot wax melts the glue holding it together. Tape around the outside of the box as well.

2 Attach the wick to the wick sustainer as usual and apply a small ball of wax glue to the bottom of the sustainer. With a tall box like this, you will need to use a skewer to press the sustainer down onto the bottom of the box.

3 Make the candle as for the dessert cup mold above, using a quantity of wax and size of wick suitable for your mold (see pages 10 and 16). When the candle is completely cool, remove the tape and simply tear the box off the candle.

ornate turquoise pillar

A dreamy aqua-colored wax is used for this classical pillar candle with its pleasing surface design. There are many different designs of latex mold to choose from, but these pillars are the easiest for a beginner.

you will need

- Latex candle mold, approximately 4½in (11cm) tall and 2in (5cm) diameter

- Vegetable oil (or mold release) and a brush

- Paper towel

- Wicking needle

- Wick for a 2in (5cm) diameter candle, 6in (15cm) long, primed

- Wick holder

- Mold seal

- 7oz (200g) paraffin wax

- 1 level teaspoon Vybar

- Blue and green wax dye

- Wax melting pan

- Thermometer

- Cardboard mold support (see page 14)

- Container to hold the mold support and the mold

- Skewer

 **timing** 30 minutes plus cooling time

tip You will need to pull quite hard on the mold to remove it from the candle, but be careful not to tear the latex or snap the candle.

1 Turn the latex mold inside out and brush over the inside with vegetable oil, working the oil into the crevices. Mop away any excess with a paper towel so that it cannot spoil the surface of the molded candle. Turn the mold right side out.

2 Thread the needle with one end of the primed wick and push the needle through the top of the candle mold from the inside. If this is the first time that you are using the mold, you will need to make a hole in the latex.

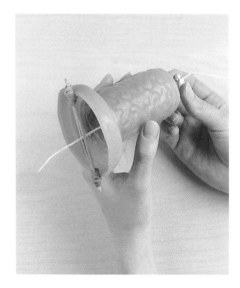

3 Clip the other end of the wick in a wick holder and pull the wick down until the holder rests on the top of the mold and the wick is held straight inside. Seal around the wick with mold seal where it emerges from the mold.

4 Melt the wax with the Vybar and add equal quantities of blue and green dye to tint the wax a pale turquoise. When the wax reaches 175°F (80°C), pour it into the mold right up to the top of the patterned area.

continued ▶

 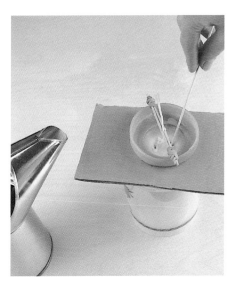 

5 Pinch all over the outside of the mold to dispel any air bubbles. Place the mold in its support and set it in a container to cool. You can fill the container with water if you wish to speed cooling but this is not essential.

6 When the wax has cooled for about 15 minutes and the center has sunk, pierce around the wick with a skewer. Top off to the original level with more wax at 175°F (80°C). When the mold has cooled again, top off once more if necessary and leave to cool thoroughly.

7 Remove the mold seal and the wick holder. Trim the wick close to the wax at the base. Smear soapy water over the outside of the mold for lubrication and pull the mold down over itself to remove it from the candle, easing it over any protruding parts. Trim the wick and flatten the base.

Latex molds allow you to make pillar candles with intricate surface detailing. It is important to pinch the mold as shown in step 5 as air bubbles can easily get trapped in the patterning of the mold.

rolled beeswax

This is a quick and easy way to make luscious beeswax candles that smell simply heavenly. Beeswax sheets have a honeycomb texture which adds to the charm of these candles. These projects are ideal for children because no molten wax is used.

continued ▶

you will need

Simple rolled candle:

- 1 sheet of natural beeswax
- Wick for a 1in (25mm) diameter candle, 10in (25cm) long, primed

Tapered candle:

- 1 sheet of natural beeswax
- Metal ruler
- Sharp knife
- Cutting board
- Wick for a 1in (25mm) diameter candle, 10in (25cm) long, primed

Small candle:

- 2 sheets of natural beeswax
- Sharp knife
- Cutting board
- Long ruler
- Wick for a 1½in (38mm) diameter candle, 4½in (12cm) long, primed

timing A simple rolled candle will take about 10 minutes to make; tapered and squat candles only slightly longer.

tip Work in a warm room because the beeswax sheets need to be warm to roll easily. A hairdryer can help to keep the wax soft and supple on a cold day.

variation Beeswax sheets come in colored versions as well as natural colors. Try rolling up two different colored sheets of slightly different sizes to make a multicolored, tapered candle.

simple rolled candle

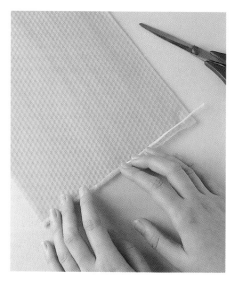

1 Lay the primed wick along the edge of one of the short sides of the beeswax sheet with one end protruding about ½in (13mm) from the sheet. Turn the first ⅛in (3mm) of the sheet over the wick and press it down tightly all along its length to enclose the wick.

2 Now roll up the sheet, keeping each roll as tight as possible and taking care to keep the edges straight or the candle will not stand level.

3 Press all along the end of the rolled sheet with your nail to attach it firmly and prevent the sheet from unrolling. Trim the wick to ½in (13mm).

tapered candle

small candle

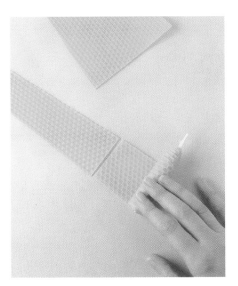

1 Lay the sheet of beeswax on a board and place a metal ruler diagonally across the sheet, offset from each corner by about ½in (13mm). Cut along the ruler with your knife. This will give you two identical sheets – enough to make two tapered candles.

2 Lay the primed wick along the base of the tapered sheet and roll up as before, rolling towards the pointed end of the sheet. Keep the straight side of the sheet as square as possible. Press firmly along the spiral edge with your nail to seal the candle.

1 Lay two sheets on your board, end to end and place a long ruler at a shallow angle across them both. The longer end should be about 4in (10cm) long and the short end about 1¼in (3cm) long. Cut along the ruler with your knife, across both sheets. The excess sheets can be used in other projects. Lay the primed wick along the longer end of the first sheet with the wick protruding from the angled end. Roll the sheet up with the wick inside as before. When you reach the end of the first sheet, butt the edge of the second sheet against it and continue rolling tightly to the end. Press the final edge onto the candle with your nail. Trim the wick to ½in (13mm). This produces an attractive domed candle.

molded candles

projects

coffee and cream tilted layers

These striking candles are made simply by layering different colored waxes into a tilted mold. Each layer is allowed to partially set before the mold is tilted at a new angle and the next layer of colored wax is poured in.

you will need

- Pillar mold, 2¾in (7cm) tall and 3in (7.5cm) diameter
- Wick for a 2½in (6cm) candle, primed
- Wick seal
- Wick holder
- Bowl filled with sand or earth, large enough to hold the mold
- 9oz (250g) paraffin wax
- 1oz (25g) stearin (2½ tbsp)
- Wax melting pan or metal pitcher
- Thermometer
- Brown wax dye, sufficient for 5½oz (150g) wax
- Skewer

timing 45 minutes plus setting time

tip This candle is easy to make because only one color of dye is used and more dye is simply added with each layer to give increasingly dark layers. For a really colorful candle, try using several contrasting colors.

1 Insert the wick into the mold (see page 29) and seal and clip it in place. Set the mold into the bowl of sand so that it is at an angle and held firmly.

2 Melt the wax and stearin but add no dye at this point because the first layer is white wax. When the wax reaches 175°F (80°C), pour some into the mold to fill it about one-third full. The top level will lie across the mold at an angle.

3 Leave the candle to set until the top surface has formed a thick layer that will only just bend when pressed with your finger. Tip the mold in the opposite direction and settle it in the sand again. Watch the surface as you do this – if the wax is still too soft, it will bulge and sag.

4 Reheat the remaining wax and add enough dye to give a light brown color. When the wax reaches 175°F (80°C), pour it into the mold to reach about ⅜in (1cm) from the top on the lower side. Leave to set as before.

5 When the surface of the new wax is firm to the touch, reheat the wax with the remaining brown dye to make a darker shade of brown. Set the mold level and fill to the top with the dark brown wax heated to 175°F (80°C).

6 When the candle has cooled and the surface sunk, pierce the center with a skewer and top off with more dark brown wax. Leave to cool completely then remove from the mold. Trim the wick to ½in (13mm) and flatten the base if need be.

star cubes

Pastel shapes speckle the sides of these pretty cube candles. Candles with embedded squares of

wax are always popular, but this project gives a sparkling variation with cut-out shapes embedded

in the white wax. You can try different colors and shapes using any small cutters.

you will need

- Aluminum foil
- Shallow dish
- 2oz (50g) paraffin wax for the stars
- 1 tsp microcrystalline hard
- Wax melting pan or metal pitcher
- Blue wax dye
- Star cutters: ½in (13mm) and ⅜in (10mm)
- Cube mold, 3in (8cm) tall and 2in (5cm) across
- Wick for a 2in (50mm) diameter candle, primed
- Wick seal
- Wick holder
- 7oz (200g) paraffin wax
- 2 tbsp (20g) stearin
- Thermometer
- Water bath
- Skewer

timing 45 minutes plus cooling time.

tip Microcrystalline hard wax is used to make the stars so that they will not melt when the white wax is poured into the mold. If you do not have this hard wax, use extra stearin instead (up to 20 percent of the wax quantity).

1 Shape a 4in (10cm) square of foil into a shallow tray by turning up the sides ⅝in (1.5cm) and pinching the corners to hold it in shape. Place it in a shallow dish in case it leaks.

2 Melt the microcrystalline hard in a saucepan or pitcher over a direct heat. Stir in 2oz (50g) paraffin wax with a little blue dye to make a pale blue. Pour the melted wax into the foil tray and leave to cool until it is firm but still flexible.

3 Peel the slab of wax off the foil. Working quickly so that the wax does not become too hard to cut, use the cutters to cut out about 12 stars.

4 Briefly press each star on the base of a pan to flatten one side and melt a little, then quickly press onto the inside of the cube so the molten wax makes it stick. Make a starry pattern over all four sides.

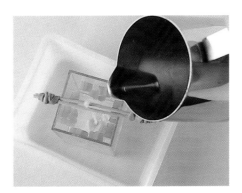

5 Secure the wick in the mold in the usual way, taking care not to dislodge any stars. Melt the 7oz (200g) of paraffin wax with the stearin until it reaches 175°F (80°C). Pour into the mold to reach about ¼in (6mm) from the top. Immediately place the mold in a water bath to prevent the stars from melting.

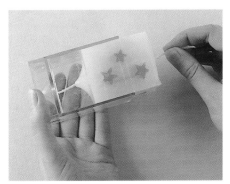

6 When the wax has cooled and sunk in the center, pierce and top off in the usual way. When the candle is completely cool, slide it out of the mold, then trim the wick and flatten the base.

splash candle

Hot wax drizzled into cold water produces wonderful random threads and whirls of wax. This project uses the water-cooled wax as an inclusion to make an unusual, rough textured candle.

you will need

- 2oz (50g) paraffin wax
- 1 tsp micro-crystalline hard
- Blue and yellow wax dyes
- Wax melting pan or metal pitcher
- Bowl of cold water
- Cloth towel
- Pillar mold, 2½in (7cm) tall and 2½in (7cm) across

- Wick for a 2½in (7cm) diameter candle, primed
- Wick holder
- Wick seal
- 7oz (200g) paraffin wax
- 2 tbsp (20g) stearin
- Thermometer
- Water bath

timing 30 minutes plus cooling time.

tip Microcrystalline hard is added to the colored wax to make the splashed strands stronger and less likely to melt away when the hot wax is poured onto them.

1 Melt the 2oz (50g) of wax with the microcrystalline hard and enough dye to make a strong blue. Using a pitcher with a good spout, drizzle half of the wax in a fine stream over the surface of the bowl of water. It will harden at once into rippling threads of wax. Scoop these off the surface of the water onto a cloth towel to dry.

2 Add yellow dye to the remaining blue wax to color it green and repeat to make green drizzled strands.

3 Insert the wick into the mold and seal as usual. Fill the mold with the colored wax threads, packing them around the wick. You can make colored layers, or a random mix of color.

4 Melt the 7oz (200g) of paraffin wax with the stearin. When the wax temperature reaches 180°F (82°C), pour it into the mold over the strands, filling to just below the top. You can use a water bath at this point to speed the cooling.

5 When the wax has cooled and shrunk around the wick, top off with more wax at 175°F (80°C). The wax will cool faster than normal because of the wax strands. Cool thoroughly and then unmold. Trim the wick and flatten the candle base.

ice candle

Easy to make and resembling colored Swiss cheese, ice candles are remarkably beautiful as they burn down. Hot wax is poured into a mold full of crushed ice; the wax sets around the ice which melts away to leave spectacular holes and hollows. Here, a plain white candle is used as a core candle to ensure successful burning.

you will need

- 2 pint (1 litre) size rectangular waxed cardboard juice carton
- Sharp scissors
- Sticky tape
- Sharp knife
- Cutting board
- 6in (15cm) plain white candle
- Approximately 1 pint (500ml) ice cubes
- An old towel
- Hammer
- 11oz (300g) paraffin wax
- 1oz (30g) stearin (3 tbsp)
- Violet wax dye
- Wax melting pan or metal pitcher
- Thermometer
- Bowl

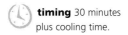 **timing** 30 minutes plus cooling time.

tip An orange juice carton is used in this project but you could use a rigid candle mold instead. The best ice holes occur at the bottom of the mold so this candle is made with the top facing down, as with purchased molds.

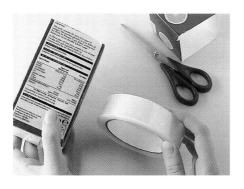

1 Cut off the top of the carton about 5in (13cm) from the base. Thoroughly wash out and dry the inside of the carton. Tape around the joins of the carton with sticky tape.

2 Using a sharp knife and cutting board, carefully trim around the top of the household candle to flatten it slightly and expose more wick. Cut off the bottom of the candle so that when placed inside the carton, it reaches to ¾in (2cm) below the top edges.

3 Wrap the ice cubes in the towel and carefully use the hammer to break them into smaller pieces. The ideal size is ¾in (2cm) with smaller chippings as well.

4 Stand the core candle, top down, in the center of the carton and pack the ice pieces around it to hold it upright. The ice should just reach the level of the core candle's base.

5 Melt the wax and stearin with enough dye to make a pale violet and heat it to 210°F (100°C). Standing the mold in a bowl in case of leaks, pour in the hot wax, filling it to just above the base of the core candle.

6 Leave the candle to set for at least one hour (there is no need to top off). Hold the candle over the bowl to catch the melted ice and tear off the mold. Pull the wick clear of the wax at the top of the candle and leave it to dry out overnight before lighting.

frosted floating stars

Floating candles always have a particular magic, perhaps because they combine fire and water in such a charming way. These little star candles are decorated with pearl powder, glitter and sequins to great effect and will burn for at least one and a half hours.

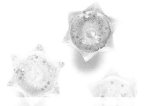

you will need

For six floating candles, 2in (5cm) across the points and 1in (2.5cm) deep:

- Mold for star floating candles
- ½ teaspoon microcrystalline hard (optional)
- Wax melting pan or metal pitcher
- 3½oz (100g) paraffin wax
- 1 tbsp (10g) stearin

- Thermometer
- Small pitcher
- Skewer
- Wick for 1in (25mm) diameter candles, primed and cut into six 1½in (4cm) lengths
- Pearl powder
- Small paintbrush
- Fine frosted glitter
- Craft glue
- Tiny star sequins

timing 30 minutes plus setting time

tip Floating candle molds are available in many shapes including the stars used here. A special mold is not necessary to make floating candles – wax floats on water so any small candle that is wider than it is tall can be used as a floating candle.

1 If you are using microcrystalline hard wax, melt this first in the bottom of the pan over a direct heat. Add the paraffin wax and stearin and melt all together until the temperature reaches 175°F (80°C). Using a small pitcher so that you can pour accurately, fill each mold cavity to just below the top. Set the mold aside to cool.

2 When the center of each candle has sunk and the surface has formed a thick skin, pierce the center of each candle with a skewer and immediately push a wick into the center. Leave to cool for another 10 minutes.

3 Top off each little candle with more wax heated to 175°F (80°C). The fresh wax will form a circular pool in the center of each candle. If the wicks start to topple, leave them to cool for a few minutes then pull them upright or prop them up with a skewer.

4 When the candles are completely cool, remove them from the molds. Heat a pan and rub the base of each candle on the bottom of the pan to melt the wax slightly. This seals the wick so water cannot enter and make the candle sputter or go out. Trim the wicks.

5 Brush over the surface of each candle with pearly powder and sprinkle on a little glitter. Use craft glue to glue a scatter of sequins across the top of each candle.

pine hurricane shell

This spectacular candle is a wax shell with embedded pine needles and cones. A small tea light or votive is burned inside and this illuminates the shell to give a glorious atmospheric glow on a window sill or as a table centerpiece.

you will need

- Vegetable oil and brush
- Plastic bowl or ice-cream tub, approximately 6in (15cm) diameter
- Smaller diameter plastic bowl, approximately 4in (10cm) diameter
- Paper towel
- 1lb (450g) uncolored paraffin wax
- Wax melting pan or metal pitcher
- Thermometer
- Small branches of pine needles
- Several small pine cones, cut in half lengthwise
- Skewer
- Aluminum foil
- Tea light or votive

 **timing** 45 minutes plus cooling time

tip Fresh pine is preserved in the wax and the shell will last for several months. You can also include dried or silk flowers but avoid fresh flowers which will rot inside the wax.

1 Brush a thin layer of oil over the inside of the large bowl and mop away any excess with paper towel. Oil the outside of the small bowl in the same way.

2 Heat the wax to 175°F (80°C) and pour a ¼in (5mm) thick layer into the bottom of the large bowl. Leave to cool and set.

3 Stand the small bowl in the center of the large bowl, on the cooled wax layer. Push the pine branches into the gap between the two bowls and tuck the halved pine cones amongst the needles, with the cut side facing inwards.

4 Fill the small bowl with cold water to weigh it down. Reheat the wax to 175°F (80°C) and pour it into the pine-filled space between the bowls to just below the outer bowl rim. Use a skewer to push the foliage down if it floats.

5 After about 20 minutes, the center of the wax surface between the bowls will have sunk. Pierce through this into the molten center and top off with more hot wax in the same way as topping off a candle. Repeat when the wax has cooled further.

6 Leave the shell to cool completely, then remove the center bowl and pull the shell out of the outer bowl. Flatten the top edge of the shell by pressing it down onto some foil that has been laid in the bottom of a heated pan. To display the shell, place it on a heatproof surface and set a small tea light or votive inside the shell.

frosted pyramid

Intriguing swirls and ripples embellish the surface of these unusual candles. The effect is simply

the result of pouring the wax into the mold just as it reaches setting point. You will need to use a

rigid mold to get the full benefit of this technique.

you will need

- Pyramid candle mold, 8in (20cm) tall and 2in (5cm) across the base
- Wick for a 1in (25mm) diameter candle, primed
- Mold seal
- Wick holder
- 7oz (200g) paraffin wax
- 2 tbsp (20g) stearin
- Red and blue wax dye
- Wax melting pan or metal pitcher
- Thermometer
- Tablespoon
- Skewer

timing 30 minutes plus cooling time.

tip This rippled effect works best with mid- or dark-colored wax. The technique usually leaves patches of wax on the inside of the mold so clean it well after use (see page 19).

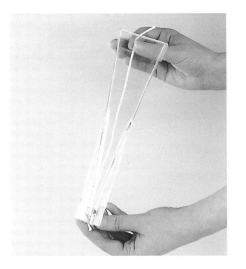

1 Insert the wick into the mold and seal it with mold seal. Clip the other end of the wick in the wick holder. Melt the wax and stearin with the red dye and a little blue to make a rich burgundy.

2 Leave the wax to cool in the pan, monitoring the temperature, until it drops to about 150°F (65°C) and a thin skin starts to form over the surface.

3 Pour about 2 tablespoons of wax into the mold and, holding the mold over the wax pan, slowly turn the mold so the wax swirls all over the inside to make a thin covering. Pour any remaining wax back into the pan.

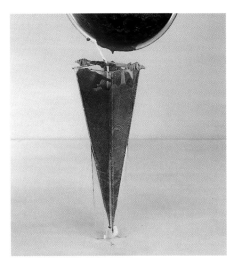

4 Allow the wax in the pan to cool for a few minutes more, stirring it gently. Then pour it into the mold, filling it to the top as usual. Leave to cool and pierce and top off as usual.

5 When the candle is completely cool, remove the mold seal and the wick holder and slide the candle out of the mold. The swirls of the cooling wax will have left wonderful natural patterns on the sides of the candle. Trim the wick and flatten the candle's base (see page 19).

ivy leaves

Dreamy images of silk ivy leaves are visible through the wax in this appealing candle. A central core candle is used so that the flame burns down in a cavity in the center of the candle, away from the leaves.

you will need

- Pillar candle mold, 4in (10cm) tall and 2½in (6cm) diameter at the base
- Vegetable oil and brush
- Paper towel
- Plain white candle, ¾in (20mm) thick, trimmed to 3½in (9cm) long
- Mold seal
- Wick holder
- Sprig of variegated silk ivy leaves
- 7oz (200g) paraffin wax
- Wax melting pan or metal pitcher
- Thermometer
- Skewer
- Water bath

timing 45 minutes plus cooling time.

tip No stearin is used in this candle so the candle is as translucent as possible. A transparent plastic mold makes it easier to see the effect of the included leaves while you are making the candle.

1 Brush over the inside of the mold with vegetable oil and mop away the excess with paper towel. The oil will make the candle easy to remove despite the lack of stearin.

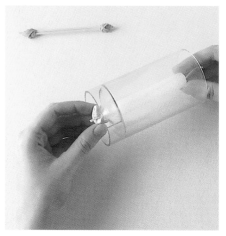

2 Push the wick of the plain candle through the wick hole in the mold and seal with mold seal. The candle should be about ⅜in (1cm) shorter than the mold. Keep the wick in place with a wick holder.

3 Cut two small sprigs of ivy leaves and push them into the space between the side of the mold and the core candle. Arrange them to make an attractive effect when seen through the sides of the mold. Melt the wax and heat it until it reaches 175°F (80°C).

4 Pour the hot wax into the mold. Use a skewer to push down the ivy leaves if they try to float, pressing them against the sides of the mold to ensure that they will be visible through the wax when the candle has set. Make sure that the core candle is central.

5 Place the mold in a water bath to speed cooling. When the wax has cooled and sunk, pierce around the core candle and top off with more hot wax in the usual way. When the candle is completely cool, remove the mold seal and slide it out of the mold. It should come out easily, sliding against the oil. Wipe away any remaining oil, trim the wick and flatten the candle base.

waterglass candle

This charming candle is ideal for a dinner party table. A small candle floats on the water in a

drinking glass and its glow lights up objects in the water below. You can fill the glass with anything

you like, from fresh flowers and fruit to glass nuggets or pebbles. The glass itself is used as the

candle mold to ensure that the candle fits perfectly.

you will need

- Tall straight-sided drinking glass
- Vegetable oil and brush
- Wick for a 1in (25mm) candle, primed, and long enough to reach from the base of the glass to 1in (25mm) above the rim
- Wick sustainer
- Pliers
- Wax glue
- Long skewer
- Wick holder
- 2oz (50g) paraffin wax
- ½ tbsp (5g) stearin
- Wax melting pan or metal pitcher
- Thermometer
- Pebbles to place in the glass
- Denatured alcohol, optional

 **timing** 30 minutes plus setting time

tip The candle is molded in the bottom of the glass so you will need a very long piece of wick when making the candle. The leftover wick can be reused in other projects.

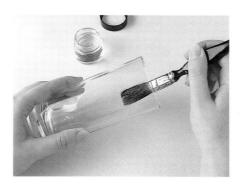

1 Brush over the inside of the bottom half of the glass with vegetable oil. This will help to release the candle when it is cold. Attach one end of the wick to the wick sustainer.

2 Apply wax glue to the bottom of the sustainer and use a long skewer to press this onto the bottom of the glass. Clip the other end of the wick in the wick holder and pull the wick holder down the wick until it rests on the glass rim.

3 Melt the wax with the stearin and heat to 175°F (80°C). Pour wax into the bottom of the glass to a depth of about 1¼in (3cm). Avoid splashing wax on the sides of the glass or the candle will be difficult to remove when cold.

4 Leave the candle to cool until it has partly set and the area around the wick has sunk. Pierce round the wick with a skewer and top up with more 175°F (80°C) wax. Pour in the topping-off wax so that it makes a neat circle around the wick.

5 Leave the candle to cool completely. The stearin will make it shrink away from the sides of the glass when it is cold. Pull gently on the wick to slide the candle out of the glass.

6 Trim the wick to ⅜in (10mm) long. Wash the glass with soapy water to remove the oil. If necessary, clean away any traces of wax with denatured alcohol. Fill the glass with pebbles, add water to 2in (5cm) below the rim and float the candle on the water.

multiwick candle

Large diameter candles have a pleasing, block effect and burn best with several small wicks spaced evenly rather than one large wick in the center. This project shows you how to make cardboard molds for these big candles.

you will need

- Template (see page 138)

- Thick cardboard, 8 x 10in (20 x 25cm)

- Straight edge

- Cutting board

- Heavy-duty craft knife

- Clear tape

- Wax melting pan or metal pitcher

- 1oz (25g) stearin (2½ tbsp)

- Green and blue wax dye

- 9oz (250g) paraffin wax

- Thermometer

- Container (to hold the mold)

- Ruler and pencil

- Hand drill (or electric drill) with a ⅛in (3mm) drill bit

- Long metal skewer

- Wick for a 1in (25mm) diameter candle, cut into three 2¼in (6cm) lengths and primed

timing 60 minutes plus cooling time

tip Use any kind of stiff cardboard for this project – the sides of a corrugated cardboard grocery carton are ideal.

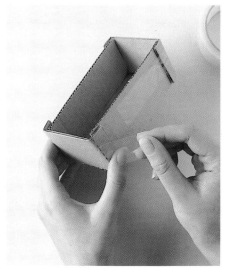

1 Trace the template on page 138 onto the cardboard. Use the straight edge, cutting board and the knife to cut it out along the cutting lines. Score with the back of the knife along the folding lines.

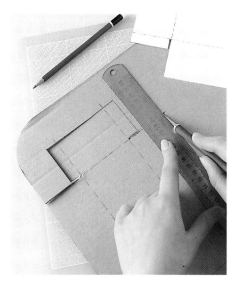

2 With the scored lines to the outside, bend up the sides of the mold and bend the flaps at the sides of the short ends round onto the long sides. Tape the flaps down and tape all along the joins and folds.

3 In the pan, melt the stearin with the green dye and a little blue dye to make a dark turquoise. Add the wax and continue heating until the temperature reaches 160°F (70°C). Place the mold in a container to catch any leaks and pour the wax into the mold to within ⅜in (1cm) of the top.

4 When the wax has cooled enough to sink in the center, pierce and top up in the usual way. Cool and top up again until the candle sets with a flat surface.

continued ▶

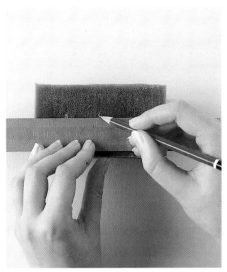

5 Remove the tape from the mold and ease the mold away from the candle. If you are careful when you remove the mold, you should be able to re-use it several times.

6 Turn the block over so that the smooth bottom becomes the top of the candle. Lay the ruler along the center line of the block and make a mark with the pencil every 1¼in (3cm) to mark the position of the three wicks.

7 Working on a suitable surface, use the hand drill to make a hole at each of the marks. Hold the drill as vertically as possible and take care not to damage the wax surface around the holes. Brush away the loose wax.

8 If the drill bit is not long enough to make a hole right through the candle, heat a metal skewer over a candle flame and push it down the hole to melt it right through. Push the primed wicks into the wick holes and trim them to ½in (13mm). When the wicks are lit, they will melt the surrounding wax slightly and seal themselves into the holes.

yin yang candle

The ancient symbols of harmony and the balance of opposites, Yin and Yang, make a striking pair of candles. Chocolate brown and pearl white dyes are used to give a strong color contrast.

continued ▶

you will need

- Aluminum foil
- Strip of thin card, 6½ x 2in (17 x 5cm)
- Scissors
- A straight-sided cake tin or pot for the mold, inside measurement approximately 4in (10cm) diameter and 2in (5cm) high
- Masking tape
- Vegetable oil and brush
- 11oz (300g) paraffin wax
- 2 wax melting pans or metal pitchers
- Pearl white and chocolate brown wax dye
- 30g (1oz) stearin (3 tbsp)
- Thermometer
- Skewer
- Wick for a 2in (50mm) candle, cut into two 3in (8cm) lengths and primed
- Two wick holders
- Sharp knife

 **timing** 45 minutes plus cooling time.

tip You can use any straight-sided round container for this project and vary the size of your Yin and Yang candles.

1 Cut a piece of foil just longer than the card and twice as wide. Fold it in half lengthwise and insert the card to make a foil-wrapped divider.

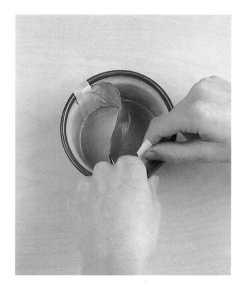

2 Bend the divider into an 'S' shape and, with the folded side down, position it inside the tin to divide the circle into the two Yin and Yang shapes. Tape the two ends firmly to the sides of the pot.

3 Brush all over the inside of the pot and the divider with oil. Melt 2oz (50g) of the paraffin wax and pour it into the pot to make a layer about 5mm (¼in). It will flow under the divider to reach the same level on both sides and seal the divider in place. Leave to cool until firm.

4 Pearl white dye needs a high temperature to melt, so cut it into small slivers and put into a pan with a tablespoon of wax. Heat over a direct heat until it is melted. Add half the wax and half the stearin and heat to 175°F (80°C).

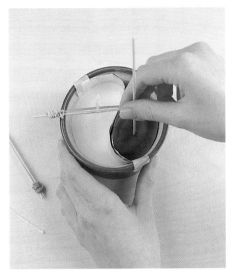

5 In a separate pan, dye the remaining wax and stearin dark brown in the usual way and heat to the same temperature. Pour the pearl white wax into one half of the mold, filling to just below the top. Immediately pour the brown wax into the other half, up to the same level.

6 Leave the wax to cool until a layer has formed over the surface about ⅛in (3mm) thick. Pierce a hole in the center of the widest part of each half and insert a length of primed wick. Use two wick holders to keep the wicks upright.

7 When the wax has cooled further and the center of the candle has sunk, pierce around the wicks and top each half off at the original level with hot wax in their respective colors. You may need to do this once more. Leave the mold to cool completely.

8 Pull the tape away from the mold and lift the candle out by pulling gently on the wicks. You may need to insert a knife around the edges to free the taped part. Remove all the tape. Make a vertical cut where each color of wax tapers against the other to trim away the thin ends of the Yin and Yang 'tails'.

9 Turn the candle over – the 'S' shaped line that is the bottom of the divider will be visible through the wax. Score along the line with a sharp knife and pull the two halves apart. Remove the divider and trim away any rough edges. Finally trim the wicks to ½in (13mm).

pine cone candles

Pine cone candles have great appeal, particularly when made in smoky colors and scented with pine essential oil. This project shows you how to make the molds for these using latex. While the actual making is not particularly time-consuming, you need to allow time for both the clay and then the latex to dry before you can make the candle.

you will need

To make the mold:

- 1lb (500g) air drying clay
- A small board or tile to work on
- A few simple sculpting tools (you can improvise with a table knife and a knitting needle)
- 3½oz (100ml) latex
- An old paintbrush
- Talcum powder
- Sharp scissors

To make the candle:

- Wick for a 1in (25mm) diameter candle, primed
- Wick seal
- Wick holder
- 4oz (100g) paraffin wax
- ½ teaspoon Vybar
- Purple or green wax dye, plus a trace of black to make smoky colors
- 5 drops of pine or cedar essential oil

timing Sculpting the pine cone in clay: 1 hour plus two days drying time

Making the mold: a few minutes every 10 minutes or so for approximately two hours to allow drying between layers. 2–3 hours drying time

Molding the candle: 1 hour including setting time.

tip Liquid latex is available from candlemaking suppliers or sculpting suppliers

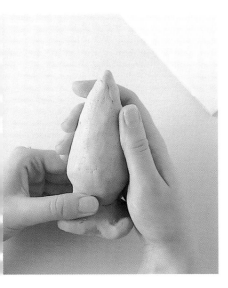

1 To make the mold master, shape soft clay into a cone about 4½in (12cm) high and 2¼in (6cm) across at the base. Squeeze with both hands about 1in (2.5cm) above the base to narrow the clay into a waist. Set the cone onto the board and, using your hands, refine the shape into a smooth pine cone.

2 Use a knife to mark diagonal lines all over the surface of the cone. The lines should be close together at the top and wider apart at the base. If you have a real pine cone, use this as a guide.

3 Now sculpt the diamond shapes between the lines into the pine cone scales. This cone is from a Scots pine and has quite textured scales but you can leave the scales smoother if you wish.

continued ▶

4 Refine the base of the model. The waist should not go in by more than ⅜in (1cm) all round, or the mold will be hard to remove from the candle. Shape the base into a rough rectangle – this will form the mold's flange. Place the model, still on its board, in a warm room for several days until it is completely dry.

5 Heat the clay model in a cool oven at 200°F (100°C/gas mark ⅛) for 20 minutes. Remove it from the oven and immediately brush all over the surface with latex, using an old brush. The warm, dry clay will absorb the moisture in the latex and make a thick first layer. Brush out the bubbles that form on the surface.

6 After about 5–10 minutes, the first layer will have set and the creamy color partly changed to tan. Brush on another layer of latex, as thickly as possible without it dripping.

7 Continue in this way, allowing each layer to dry before applying the next. You will need 8–10 layers for the mold to be strong enough for candlemaking. Keep your brush in water between applying layers.

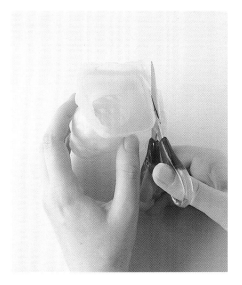

Tips for Making Latex Molds

• Latex is a non-toxic liquid rubber but should be used with care. Do not spill on clothes or fabrics because it will be impossible to remove. Work in a well-ventilated room.

• Always use an old brush to paint latex – you will not be able to clean it thoroughly after use. Place the brush in water between applications to prevent it from drying out.

• Latex should be poured into a small bowl before use. Cover this with cling wrap between applications to prevent drying out.

• Air drying clay and plaster of Paris are the easiest masters to use when making a latex mold. You can use non-porous masters such as wood or even actual fruit and vegetables but it is harder to build up the layers of latex.

• Latex thickener is available to add to latex to make the layers build up faster. This is useful when using non-porous masters.

8 When the final layer has been painted on, leave the mold to set for 3 hours or overnight. Dust the surface of the mold with talcum powder and carefully ease it off the clay model.

9 Trim the edge of the mold with sharp scissors. The mold is now ready to use, so follow the instructions on page 35 for making a candle with a latex mold. You can scent pine cone candles with cedar or pine essential oils and color them dark green or dusky purple for a fragrant display.

Try sculpting other clay shapes to make latex molds. These pebble molds are easy to make and the finished candles have a whimsical appeal when displayed and lit amongst real pebbles in a bowl.

andles

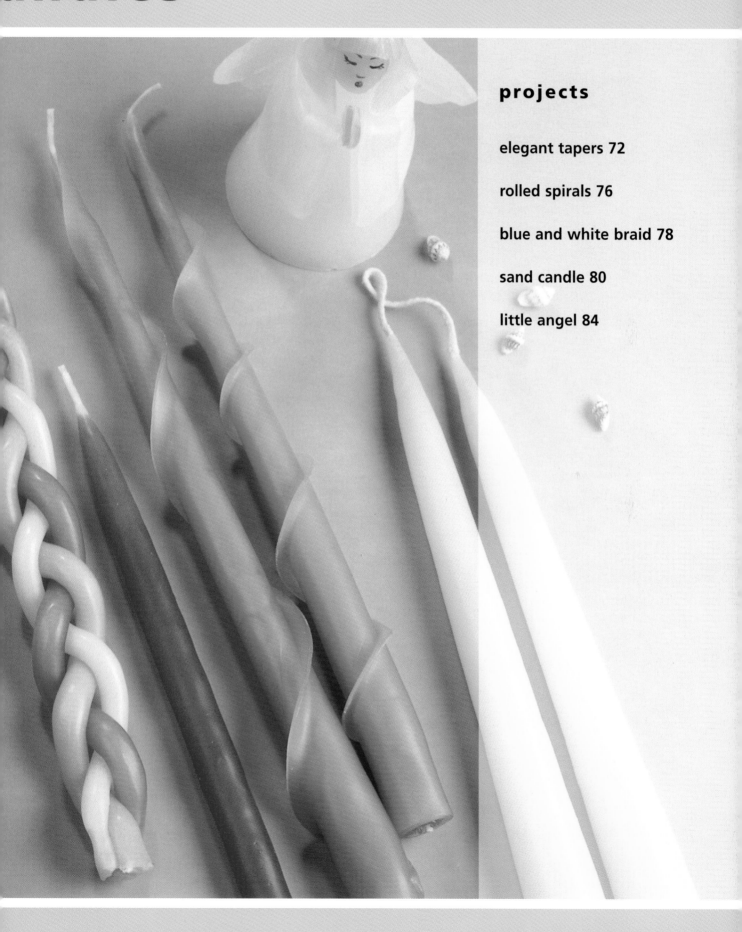

projects

elegant tapers

This is the traditional method for making slim, elegant tapers. Four candles (or more) are made

at a time and there is no need to melt huge quantities of wax to fill a dipping can – here, the can

is filled with hot water and a layer of molten wax is floated on the surface. When the wicks are

dipped repeatedly, the wax builds up just as well as when the can contains only melted wax.

you will need

To make four 8in (20cm) tapers:

- Pliers

- Wire coathanger or 32in (80cm) of strong galvanized wire

- 56in (140cm) wick for 1in (25mm) diameter candles

- Cardboard grocery box, at least 12in (30cm) deep

- Dipping can at least 12in (30cm) tall

- Hot water to fill the dipping can to within 2in (5cm) of the top

- Thermometer

- Wax melting pan or metal pitcher

- 11oz (300g) paraffin wax

- Wax dye in the color of your choice

- 1 tsp microcrystalline hard (optional)

timing About 30 minutes to make four tapers, depending on room temperature.

tip If you make two or more dipping frames, you can make many more tapers at a time, dipping each frame of four tapers in rotation while you rest the others on the box.

tip When you have finished dipping candles, let the dipping can cool overnight. The wax will set into a hard skin on the top of the water in the can. Cut round the edge of the wax and lift it off the water. Leave this to dry thoroughly before storing it for future use (any water left in the wax will spit when heated).

1 To make a dipping frame, use the pliers to bend the coathanger or wire into a rough rectangle 12in (30cm) long and 3in (8cm) wide.

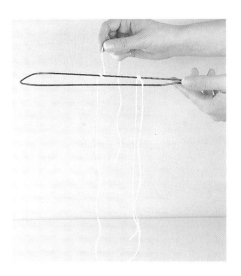

2 Cut two 28in (70cm) lengths of wick and lay the center of one across the wire frame, winding one end round the wire to secure it. The two ends should hang down about 12in (30cm) on either side of the frame. Repeat with a second length of wick, placed about 4in (10cm) away from the first.

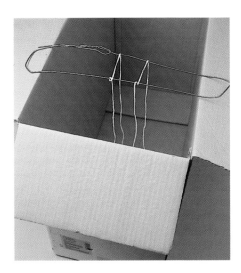

3 Lay the dipping frame across the top of the cardboard box and check that the ends of the wick hang down inside the box without touching the bottom. This is where you will rest the candles between dips to allow them to cool.

4 Place the dipping can directly on the burner and fill it with hot water of approximately 160–170°F (70–76°C). You will need to maintain this temperature throughout the dipping. Melt the wax with the dye and microcrystalline hard (if used) and pour it onto the top of the hot water in the dipping can where it will form a floating layer.

continued ▶

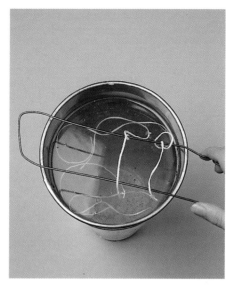

5 Hold the dipping frame above the wax and lower the wicks into it. They will float on the surface, absorbing wax. When they stop bubbling, lift them out of the wax and hold them above the can until they stop dripping. Place the frame on the box with the wicks hanging inside for several minutes until the wicks have cooled and stiffened.

6 Hold the frame above the wax again and in one swift movement, lower the wicks into the dipping can and then bring them out again. This whole action should take a maximum of two to three seconds. Lay the frame across the box for about 30 seconds for the wicks to cool.

7 Repeat step 6 about ten more times. The wax should now begin to build up on the wicks. If it does not build up, the wax may be too hot, or you are holding the wicks in the dipping can too long. If drips of wax form on the outside of the candles, the wax is too cool.

8 Continue dipping and the traditional tapered candle shape will soon appear. You will need to heat the can periodically to maintain the correct dipping temperature. Long drips will form at the bottom of each candle and you can trim these off with scissors if they touch the bottom of the box.

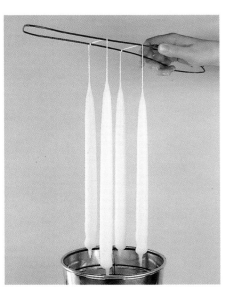

9 After 30 or more dips, the candles will reach a diameter of about ¾in (2cm). The wax layer in the dipping can will gradually be used up as you dip; top it off with more hot wax if it becomes less than ⅛in (3mm) thick.

10 When the candles have reached the thickness you want, trim the bases with scissors and hang them on the frame in the box to cool. They will be very limp at first and then harden into rigid tapers. If you want your candles to have a shiny surface, give them a final dip in cold water immediately after the last dip into the wax.

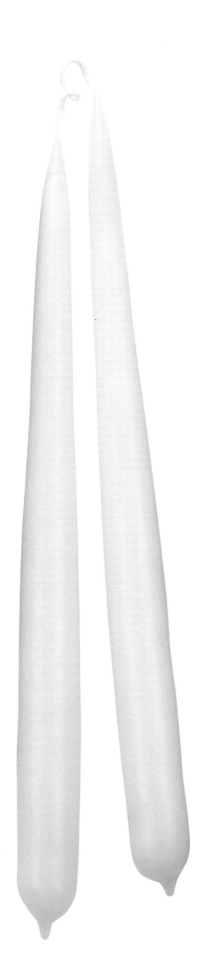

Troubleshooting for Dipped Candles

The candles begin to show thinner areas or 'waists' while dipping = they are getting too hot and the wax is sagging, so leave them to cool in the box for 10 minutes.

Water droplets appear on the outside of the candle after a dip = wax layer on the surface of the can is getting too thin. Melt more wax and add to the can.

The wax does not build up on the candles = dipping can is too hot so allow it to cool.

Small lumps of wax appear on the outside of the candles = dipping can has become too cool so heat it up a little, watching the temperature.

Making Colored Tapers

The best way to make colored tapers is to make white tapers and then overdip them in colored wax. This uses up less wax dye and gives the candles a wonderful glow because their centers are white. If you add some microcrystalline hard to the colored wax, the candles will be less likely to drip.

To overdip white tapers:

Melt some dye in the color of your choice with a little wax and add this to the dipping can, swirling it around until it is a uniform color. Use plenty of dye to make a strong color.

Hang the white tapers on the dipping frames in the usual way and dip them into the colored wax several times to build up the strength of color you want. Leave in the box to cool thoroughly. If you start with yellow dye, you can then add blue to overdip some green candles, or red to make orange candles. If you wish to make scented candles, add the scent to the colored wax.

See page 97 for instructions on how to make graded overdipped candles.

rolled spirals

These are exciting candles to make and require a little practice, but as the results are elegant and beautiful, it is well worth the effort. Poured sheets of wax are cut to shape and rolled into slim tapers; the edges of the wax are then eased out to make stylish fins before the wax hardens.

you will need

For each 11in (28cm) taper:

- Vegetable oil
- Smooth melamine board
- 2½oz (75g) dip-and-carve wax
- Green wax dye
- Wax melting pan or metal pitcher
- Small pitcher
- Sharp knife
- Hairdryer
- 12in (30cm) length of wick for 1in (25mm) diameter candles
- Hook and clothes pin for suspending the cooling candle

timing 10–15 minutes to make each taper

tip Dip-and-carve wax is used in this project because it is less likely to crack when rolled. You could also use 2oz (50g) paraffin wax mixed with one teaspoon of microcrystalline soft instead.

tip Place two strips of wood at the edges of the board before you start pouring. This is to catch any overflowing wax.

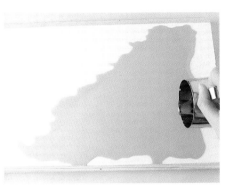

1 Rub a thin coating of oil over the board to prevent the wax from sticking. Melt the wax with a small amount of dye to make a pale green. Using a small pitcher, pour the wax onto the board in a thin stream and with a waving motion to cover a large triangular area.

2 After about 5 minutes, depending on the room temperature, the wax will have partly set into a warm sheet. Cut out as large a right-angled triangle as possible and remove the waste wax from around the edges (it can be remelted for the next candle).

3 Use the knife to slice under one end of the sheet and carefully peel it upwards to free it from the board. Lay it back on the board, ready to roll it up. If the outer edges of the wax begin to stiffen at any point, use warm air from a hairdryer to soften the wax again.

4 Lay the wick along the longer straight edge, protruding ⅜in (1cm) at each end. Bend the edge of the wax over the wick and press it down firmly to secure the wick inside. The wick needs to be held tightly in the wax so that the candle will burn well.

5 Roll the candle up tightly towards the point of the triangle, keeping the roll square to the short edge which will be the candle base. As you roll, the diagonal edge of the wax will form a spiral down the outside of the candle.

6 Hang the candle vertically from one hand and with your other hand, ease the spiral edge outwards into a smooth fin, rotating the candle as you go. Trim the base and hang the candle up by its wick to cool. Do not try to lay the candle down or the fins will be flattened.

blue and white braid

Long, thin tapers are braided together to make a stylish candle in this project. Braided candles are not difficult to make but the secret of success is to have the tapers warm and limp so that they braid easily. You can use freshly dipped tapers or simply place the tapers in water that is hot to the touch (125°F/50°C) for 15 minutes before braiding.

you will need

- 2oz (50g) paraffin wax plus one tablespoon
- Blue wax dye
- Wax melting pan
- Dipping can filled with 160°F (70°C) hot water
- Thermometer

- Three 9in (23cm) long white tapers, ⁵⁄₁₆in (15mm) thick, made using ¼in (6mm) wicks and still warm from dipping, or heated (see page 72)
- Clothes pin (or a friend to help you)
- Sharp knife

timing 30 minutes

tip Undersized wicks should be used to make the tapers for braided candles or the combined wicks will be too large and the candle will flare and smoke. See page 72 for instructions on dipping.

1 Melt the wax with the blue dye and pour it onto the top of the hot water in the dipping can. Check that the temperature is 160°F (70°C). Hold one of the tapers by its wick and give it about two dips to make it pale blue. Lay it to one side on the work surface while you dip the second candle.

2 Dip the second candle in the same way as the first but give it three or four dips to make a darker blue. Leave the third candle white.

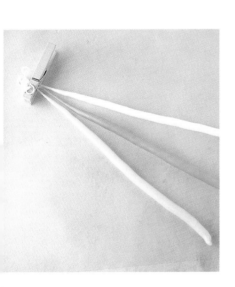

3 This step is easiest if you have someone to help you. Lay the three candles on the work surface, placing their tops together and either clip them with a clothes pin or ask someone to hold them together for you while you plait.

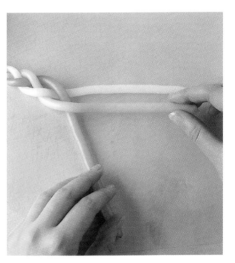

4 Now plait the candles together, bringing the right-hand candle inward over the central candle, then the left-hand candle inward over the central candle and so on.

5 When you reach the base of the candles, squeeze them together firmly. If the base is irregular, trim it off with a sharp knife. Leave the candle lying on the work surface to cool and harden.

sand candle

first saw these candles being made on a beach at Cape Cod. Shallow holes were

scooped in the damp sand for molds and the wax was melted on a driftwood fire.

But there is no need to find a beach in order to make sand candles – a bowl filled

with sand will do just as well!

you will need

- Large bowl or bucket filled with damp sand
- Small bowl, about 5in (13cm) diameter
- 1lb 2oz (500g) white paraffin wax
- Wax melting pan or metal pitcher
- Thermometer
- Metal tablespoon

- Skewers
- 3in (8cm) primed wick, 6in (15cm) long
- Scent and wax dye (optional)
- A few small seashells
- Sharp knife
- Dipping can with clear wax (optional)

timing These are quite large candles so the setting time is lengthy because you cannot speed it up with a water bath. It takes about 1 hour to make the candle but this does not include setting time.

tip If you want to make colored or scented sand candles, only add dye and scent to the last pour of wax. Otherwise the high temperatures needed for the wax will spoil the dyes and scents.

tip You can use any kind of sand for this project. Beach sand or coarse builders' sand are both fine but remove any stones larger than ³⁄₁₆in (5mm). The sand should be damp enough so that a handful will retain its shape but you cannot squeeze water out of it. Add more water or dry sand to adjust the consistency as necessary.

1 Scoop out a hole in the center of the sand, about the size of the small bowl and 2in (5cm) deep. Press the small bowl into the hole and pack the sand around it, levelling the surface.

2 Carefully ease the bowl out of the hole, taking care not to collapse the sides. The molded hole should be about 2in (5cm) deep and 5cm (13cm) across.

3 Melt the wax in a saucepan over a direct heat. Continue heating the melted wax until the temperature reaches 275°F (135°C). Do not leave the pan unattended. Hold the tablespoon in the hole and gently pour the hot wax onto the back of the spoon. This prevents the stream of wax from disturbing the sand. As the wax meets the wet sand it will hiss and bubble. After a few minutes, the bubbling will stop and the surface of the wax will have dropped about 1in (2.5cm). This is because the wax has seeped slightly into the sand before cooling and forming a shell around the candle.

continued ▶

4 Top off with more hot wax to the surface of the sand and leave the candle to cool until a rubbery surface has formed over the wax. This may take some time and depends on the temperature of the room so keep checking the candle. Pierce a hole in the center of the candle with a skewer and insert the primed wick, pushing it right down to the bottom of the candle.

5 Prop the wick with a couple of skewers laid across the top of the bowl and leave the candle to set. When the candle is nearly hard and the surface has sunk again, melt the remaining wax to 175°F (80°C). Add scent and color if you wish at this point. Top off the candle, filling it to the top of the sand surface again.

6 When the surface of the wax starts to set, place a scattering of small shells around the top of the candle. Leave the candle to set until it is completely cool (overnight is best).

7 Dig the candle out of the sand with your hands and brush off the loose sand. You will find that the sand and wax have combined to make a hard shell around the candle.

8 Use an old knife to scrape off any bumps of wax but be careful not to cut too deep or you will cut away the sandy shell. Trim the bottom of the candle, if necessary, so that it stands level.

9 Cut neatly round the top of the candle to smooth the top edge. Trim the wick to about ½in (13mm).

10 If you wish, you can overdip the candle in hot clear wax to consolidate the sandy shell. Hold the candle by its wick and dip once into hot wax on top of hot water in the dipping can (see page 79). Trim the wick.

Making Shaped Sand Candles
Once you have mastered the technique for making a simple round sand candle, you can have a lot of fun making them in different shapes. Simply press out the basic mold in the sand with a bowl and then use your hands to shape the sides into star or fish shapes. If you make three shallow holes in the bottom of the mold, these will fill with wax and the candle will stand on three legs!

little angel

Simple and appealing in translucent white, this charming candle would make a wonderful gift
for a special occasion. Sculpting with wax is not as difficult as it appears: you have to work swiftly
to shape the wax before it hardens but you can easily melt it down and try again if necessary.

you will need

- Template (see page 139)
- Tracing paper, pencil and scissors
- Wax melting pan
- Foil
- 1 molded white wax cone candle, approximately 5in (13cm) tall and 2½in (6cm) diameter at the base
- 5½oz (150g) dip-and-carve wax
- Small metal pitcher
- Red, yellow and brown wax dye discs
- Vegetable oil
- Smooth melamine board
- Hair dryer
- Sharp knife
- Wax glue
- Dark brown and red oil paints
- Fine paintbrush
- Mineral spirits

timing About 1–1½ hours to make the angel

tip If the sheets of wax become brittle when you are cutting out and handling them, use the hair dryer to soften them.

1 Trace and cut out the template pieces on page 139. Line a pan with foil and put over a low heat on the stove and press the tip of the cone candle onto the bottom of the saucepan. As the tip begins to melt, turn the candle so that all sides of the tip are melted evenly. Continue until the candle is reduced in height by about 1in (2.5cm) and has a rounded top for the top of the angel's head.

2 To make the face, melt 1oz (25g) dip-and-carve wax in a pitcher and stir in a tiny piece of red dye to make a pale flesh color. Experiment with yellow and brown dyes to make darker flesh colors. Smear a thin coating of oil onto the board and pour out some of the melted wax with a waving motion so that it makes a thin sheet on the board. Allow to cool for a few moments and then pour on a little more.

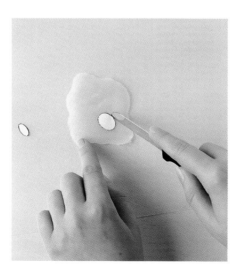

3 The wax sheet will begin to set from the edges inwards. When the center looks set and feels fairly firm to the touch but is still soft enough to mark, lay on the face template and cut around it with the point of a knife.

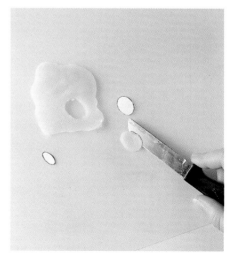

4 Pull away the scrap wax from around the shape, lift an edge of the shape with your knife, and peel it off the board.

continued ▶

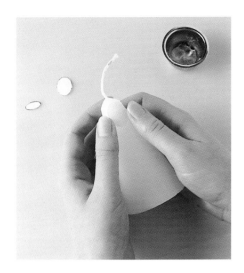

5 Apply a smear of wax glue about ¾in (2cm) from the top of the cone candle and press on the face, smoothing it down and curving it around the candle.

6 Cut out the hands shape from the pink sheet and fold the piece in half, pressing the two halves together and shaping it into a pair of praying hands. Set this aside for later.

7 To make the hair, tint another 1oz (25g) of dip-and-carve wax with tiny amounts of yellow and brown dye to make a pale straw color. Thoroughly clean the pink wax off the board and apply another smearing of oil. Pour out the straw-colored wax as for the pink wax and cut out the hair front piece.

8 Using wax glue as before, press on the hair front, overlapping the top of the face and reaching up to the wick. Use the blade of your knife to mark vertical lines on the hair front to suggest a fringe.

9 Now cut out and apply the hair back and sides in the same way. Use wax glue to stick the hair down and curve it round the back of the head, shaping it into folds round the sides of the head and overlapping the sides of the face.

10 To make the sleeves, melt the remaining 2oz (50g) of dip-and-carve wax, this time leaving it uncolored. Pour onto the oiled board and cut out the two sleeve pieces. Peel one off the board and fold back the straight edge, about 1cm (⅜in), to make a cuff.

11 Fold the sleeve in half, with the cuff to the outside. Press the curved edges together but leave the folded edge fairly open to suggest an arm inside.

12 Use a drop of wax glue to press the sleeve onto the angel's body with the cuff positioned just to one side of center and with the folded edge at the top. The sleeve should curve round to the back of the angel. Work quickly while the wax is still malleable.

13 Repeat for the other sleeve, leaving a space between the sleeves for the hands. Apply a little wax glue in the gap between the two sleeve openings and press the hands into place.

14 To make the wings, melt the white dip-and-carve wax again and pour out another sheet for the wings. Lay on the wings template and cut around it. Mark lines on the wings with your knife. Use wax glue to stick the center of the wings onto the center back. Slightly curl the wings around to the front.

15 Use the fine paintbrush and dark brown oil paint to paint eyes, brows and nose onto the face. Paint a small circle of red for the mouth. Thin some red paint with mineral spirits and dab this onto the cheeks to blush them.

decorated candles

projects

appliqué mosaic candle

Mosaics have a timeless appeal and this attractive candle combines pale yellow and green mosaic

with a fresh white background. The mosaic squares are cut from appliqué wax sheets which are

available in many different colors from candlemaking suppliers.

you will need

- Green and yellow appliqué wax sheets
- Craft knife
- Cutting board
- Ruler
- Straight edge
- Molded white globe candle, 3in (8cm) diameter

timing 1 hour approximately

tip This technique can be used on all shapes and sizes of candles and you can vary the designs and colors of the mosaic. Avoid trying to cover the entire candle with mosaic because it is very difficult to get the pieces to fit exactly.

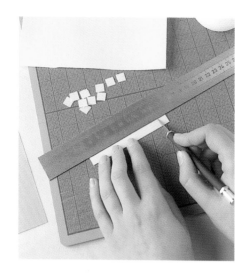

1 First cut the mosaic tiles. Place the sheet of yellow appliqué wax on a cutting surface and lay the straight edge ⅜in (1cm) in from one edge. Cut along the straight edge to make a ⅜in (1cm) wide strip. Lay the strip alongside the ruler and make marks at ⅜in (1cm) intervals all along the strip with the knife tip. Cut across the strip at each mark. This will give you lots of little square tiles for the mosaic. Repeat with the green appliqué wax.

2 Peel some of the green tiles off their paper backing and press them in a line onto the center of the globe candle at a 45-degree angle, aligning their centers with the central mold line of the globe. If they do not stick easily, press them with your fingers to warm the wax and help it to stick.

3 Continue right around the candle with the line of green tiles. To make the pattern fit, you need to have 20 tiles around the center. Now apply more green tiles in the spaces alternately above and below the first line. This will make a green zigzag right around the candle.

4 Now apply yellow tiles, following the pattern in the photographs. If your pattern does not meet at the back, just add a few extra tiles to fit.

5 Press four green tiles around the wick to finish the mosaic. Cup the globe in your hands and press the tiles on firmly all round, using the heat of your hands to mold them to the curve of the globe candle.

'cave art'

Stencilled images inspired by ancient cave paintings decorate these pleasing

candles. The textured candle surface is splattered with paint after stencilling

to suggest mottled cave walls.

you will need

- Template (see page 139)
- Thick tracing paper or stencil paper
- Sharp craft knife
- Cutting board or scrap card
- Ochre and dark brown acrylic paint
- Soft cloth or tissue

- Frosted cone candle (see page 54) made with a mix of equal quantities of orange and brown wax dye
- Masking tape
- Paintbrush or small stencil brush
- Old toothbrush

timing 30 minutes

tip You can reduce or enlarge the template on a photocopier to make different sizes of bulls to fit the dimensions of your chosen candle.

1 Trace the template on page 139 onto tracing paper. Use the craft knife to cut out the design on the cutting board. It does not matter if you do not cut very accurately because cave art can be extremely variable!

2 Smear some ochre paint onto the surface of the candle and wipe it off lightly with a soft cloth or tissue. This will leave a thin, invisible coating of paint on the candle which will help the stencilled paint to stick.

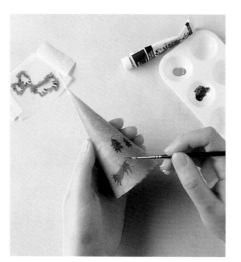

3 Tape the stencil to the candle with masking tape. Apply dark brown paint to the stencil with dabbing motions of your brush. Brush from the edge of the stencil into the center to avoid pushing paint under the stencil and smudging the outlines of the image.

4 Allow the paint to dry for about 10 minutes and then dab on another coat if necessary. Allow to dry and then remove the stencil. You may find that you will need to accentuate some parts of the design with your brush.

5 Dip an old toothbrush into the dark brown paint and stroke your finger along the bristles to spatter paint onto the candle. This will simulate the effect of the cave walls! Finally, paint a few lines under the bulls with your brush. Repeat on the other side of the candle if you wish.

pressed leaves

The delicate shapes of pressed autumn leaves decorate a classic pillar candle to suggest pages from a nature notebook. The candle used has a wick for a small diameter candle so that the flame burns down in a cavity and does not reach the outer decoration, which is then lit from within.

you will need

- Triangle and pencil
- Cream or beige tissue paper
- Fine paintbrush
- Cup of water
- Cream 2in (5cm) thick pillar candle, made with a 1in (25mm) wick
- Glue stick
- Small pressed leaves, approximately 1½in (4cm) across
- Clear wax and a dipping can (optional)

timing 45 minutes

tip Fragments of poetry can be written around the edges of the tissue paper squares instead of the simple patterns shown to make a candle with a message.

1 Use the triangle to draw four or five squares on the tissue. Vary the sizes of the squares between 1¼in (3.5cm) and 2¼in (5.5cm) across.

2 Paint a thin line of water just inside the pencil line of each square and then gently tear along the wet line. This will give a straight torn edge.

3 Draw a line of simple scallops around the sides of each square. You can vary these to make some with lines of crosses, loops or scrolls.

4 Apply glue to the back of each square and press it onto the candle. Leave space between the squares and place some on the diagonal, as though they were decorating a scrapbook.

5 Apply glue to the center of each square and press on a leaf. Some leaves will fit better if they are glued diagonally across their squares. You can overdip this candle in clear wax, if you wish, to seal the decoration.

rainbow dipped candles

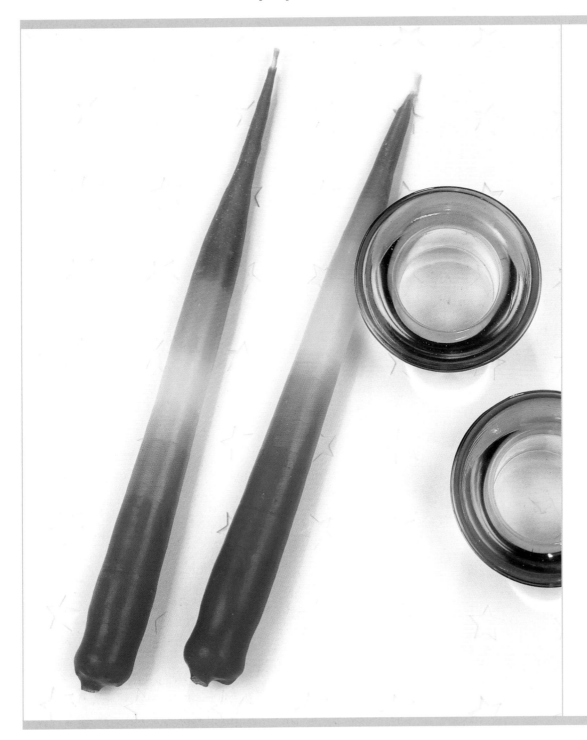

These striking candles are an entertaining exercise in color mixing, using the translucent quality of wax and only three wax colors. Plain yellow candles are overdipped with blue wax at one end and red at the other to give all the colors of the rainbow.

you will need

- 3½oz (100g) paraffin wax
- Wax melting pan or metal pitcher
- Red and blue wax dye
- Two dipping cans, each filled with 160°F (70°C) hot water
- Thermometer
- Yellow taper, 9in (23cm) long

🕐 **timing** 30 minutes

 **tip** For more subtle results, use just one color and dip only the base of the candle in graded steps.

1 Melt half the wax with enough red dye to color it a light red. Pour this onto the top of the hot water in one dipping can, checking that the temperature is 160°F (70°C). Hold the candle and dip it vertically into the red wax to about 1in (2.5cm) below the middle of the candle.

2 Now dip the candle a second time, this time to about 1 in (2.5cm) below the level of the first dip. Repeat for a third and fourth time, each dip 1in (2.5cm) less than the previous. The wax will build up on the lower part of the candle to give a color graduating from yellow through orange to red.

3 Melt the rest of the wax with some blue dye and pour this onto the top of the water in the second can. Check that the temperature is 160°F (70°C) and if it has cooled, heat the dipping can to bring it up to heat.

4 Hold the candle by the red end and dip the other end vertically into the blue wax but leave a yellow band in the center of the candle about 2in (5cm) high.

5 Make three or four more dips, as done for the red end, each dip 1in (2.5cm) less than the previous one. The blue wax will build up in steps and graduate from yellow-green to green and then blue. Lay the candle on a smooth surface to cool.

Chinese calligraphy

Chinese calligraphy has a calm simplicity and this little candle has been decorated with the symbol meaning peace or contentment. The candle is textured with a wire brush to provide contrast to the simple brush strokes.

you will need

- Template (see page 140)
- Wire brush
- Orange cube candle
- Dark brown acrylic paint
- Medium sized artists' paintbrush with a good point

timing 30 minutes

tip If you do not feel confident of painting the brush strokes evenly, trace and cut out the template to use as a stencil.

1 Using the wire brush, brush all over the surface of the candle with vertical strokes to give a pleasing streaked texture. This also gives a surface to which the paint will adhere. If you want to omit the texture, you will need to rub a thin layer of orange acrylic paint over the surface of the candle and let it dry.

2 Mix some brown paint with a little water to the consistency of thin cream. Load your brush with paint and, using the template on page 140 as a guide, make the first two small strokes at the top of the candle.

3 Make the second brush mark horizontally across the candle, ending with a slight downward curl. If you make a mistake, you can scrape the paint off gently with a knife and texture the candle again.

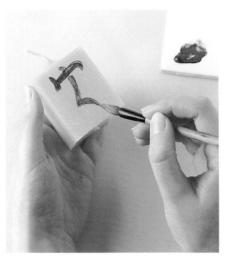

4 The third stroke runs downward and then across to the right, rather like an 'L' with the bottom line dropping down slightly. Try to make each stroke start with a slight point and finish with a neat end.

5 Finally, make the fourth and fifth strokes, like a 'T' intersecting the 'L'. If the color of the symbol is not dark enough, load your brush and go over each stroke a second time.

snowflake

These candles have been overdipped with colored microcrystalline hard to give a delicate snowflake effect. This type of wax has a high melting point and is normally added to paraffin wax to prolong a candle's burning time. Used as an overdip, it has a beautiful frosty effect once set.

you will need

- 2oz (50g) microcrystalline hard
- Blue wax dye
- Wax melting pan or metal pitcher
- Thermometer
- Dipping can filled with 175°F (80°C) hot water
- A molded white globe candle
- Pliers
- Bowl of cold water

timing 20 minutes to decorate the candle

tip Only fill the dipping can to 2in (5cm) below the top edge. A large volume candle such as this will displace a lot of water when dipped and may cause the can to overflow. The dipping temperature of microcrystalline hard needs to be 18°F (10°C) higher than that of ordinary paraffin wax.

1 Melt the microcrystalline wax with the blue dye. Pour the wax onto the surface of the hot water in the dipping can and check that the temperature is 175°F (80°C), adjusting if necessary.

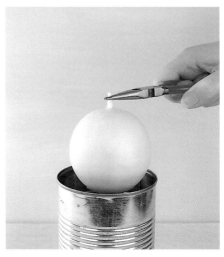

2 Hold the candle by its wick with the pliers. This will keep your fingers out of the hot wax. Dip the candle into the wax with a smooth in-and-out movement.

3 Hold the candle above the bowl of cold water and as you watch, the microcrystalline hard coating will set and white snowflake shapes will begin to appear on the surface. As soon as the snowflakes are well formed, but before they begin to join together, dip the candle into the water.

4 The cold water plunge will prevent the microcrystalline hard from whitening further. If you are not happy with the results, you can repeat the dipping and cold water plunge again.

5 Drips of wax will have formed around the base of the candle so flatten it by holding it onto the bottom of a heated saucepan for a moment.

Delft tile

The design on this delicate Delft candle comes from a paper napkin that has been applied to the candle's surface. A dip in clear wax makes the paper all but vanish, leaving a wonderful image for the candle flame to light from within. The undersized wick ensures that the flame burns down away from the decorated sides of the candle.

you will need

- Paper napkin in an attractive design
- Round white pillar candle, about 5½in (14cm) tall and 2in (5cm) diameter, made with a wick for a 1in (25mm) candle
- Scissors
- Craft glue or stick glue
- Teaspoon
- Tea light
- 3½oz (100g) paraffin wax
- Wax melting pan
- Dipping can full of 160°F (70°C) hot water

timing 30 minutes

tip Paper napkins come in an enormous variety of designs and you can use this technique to create matching candles and napkins for your party table.

1 Remove the plain backing layers of tissue from the back of the napkin. Many napkins are three-ply so be sure you remove all but the printed top layer.

2 Lay the candle on the napkin to find the size needed to wrap the candle sides neatly in the napkin without any overlaps. Cut the napkin to size.

3 Apply glue all over the sides of the candle and wrap the napkin round it, pressing it down onto the candle as tightly as possible.

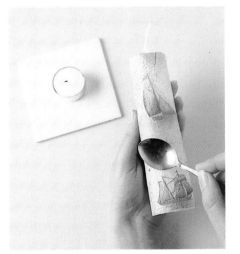

4 Heat the back of the spoon over a tea light flame, taking care not to let it become sooty in the flame. Apply the hot back of the spoon to the candle, rubbing it so that the wax melts and flows into the napkin, sticking it firmly to the candle.

5 Melt the paraffin wax and pour it onto the hot water in the dipping can. Hold the candle by the wick and dip it once into the clear wax. The wax will permeate the napkin so that it becomes barely visible. Reheat the back of the spoon and smooth out any bubbles or bumps on the candle's surface. Leave the candle to cool completely before lighting.

incised ferns

These unusual candles use a Philips screwdriver as a hot poker to incise

the design. A dark layered candle is overdipped in white wax and then the

heated screwdriver is pushed into its sides to reveal the colors below.

you will need

- 3½oz (100g) paraffin wax
- 1 tbsp (10g) stearin
- Wax melting pan
- Dipping can filled with 160°F (70°C) hot water
- Cube candle with layers of purple, dark green and blue wax
- Template (see page 140)
- Tracing paper and pencil
- Gas burner or camping gas stove (or a tea light)
- Philips screwdriver
- An old glove
- Baking sheet

timing 45 minutes plus cooling time

tip It is easiest to heat the screwdriver over a gas flame which burns clean. If you use a tea light candle, it will take longer and you must be careful not to put the screwdriver into the flame itself or it will become sooty. Wear an old glove on the hand holding the screwdriver to protect your hand from the hot wax. Do not overheat the screwdriver or its handle may begin to melt.

1 Melt the wax with the stearin and pour it onto the top of the water in the dipping can. Hold the candle by its wick and dip several times until the white wax covers the darker layers below.

2 Leave the candle to cool thoroughly. Meanwhile, trace the template from page 140 onto tracing paper. Lay the tracing onto the candle and draw over the design with the pencil to mark the lines onto the wax.

3 Put the glove on your working hand and hold the screwdriver over the gas flame for several seconds to heat it. If you are using a tea light, it will take longer to heat.

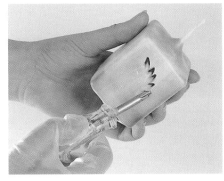

4 Hold the candle over the baking sheet to catch drips and angle the side to be decorated to face downwards. Press the screwdriver tip into the candle on one of the lines and it will melt into the wax to expose the dark colors behind it.

5 Repeat to make a series of melted marks along the marked lines of the leaf. The molten wax will run down the screwdriver and should be allowed to drip onto the baking sheet. If it does not run off the candle, it will set and spoil the design.

6 Repeat to decorate the other sides of the candle. You can try other designs as well, such as simple trees or geometric patterns.

millefiori

Millefiori candles get their name from a glassmaking technique that means 'thousand flowers'.
Patterned canes of wax, like sticks of rock, are sliced and applied to a candle to make a repeating
pattern. Commercial millefiori candles are made in a glorious variety of complex patterns that are
hard to reproduce at home. This project shows how to make a simple version with colorful spirals.

you will need

- 1oz (30g) dip-and-carve wax, dyed red
- 4oz (100g) dip-and-carve wax, uncolored
- 2 wax melting pans
- Melamine board
- Vegetable oil and brush

- Sharp knife
- A molded white egg candle with an untrimmed wick
- Wax glue
- Dipping can filled with hot water at 160°F (70°C)

timing 45 minutes

tip Use a very sharp blade to cut the wax cane so that it does not crumble. If you find it is getting too hard to cut, drop it into hot water for about 5 minutes to soften.

1 Heat the red wax until it has melted and, at the same time, melt about 1oz (30g) of the uncolored wax in another pan. Oil the board lightly and pour the red wax onto the board to make a small sheet about 4in (10cm) square. Repeat to make a similar sheet of white wax.

2 As soon as the two sheets have cooled enough to be set but still flexible, cut round each to make it into a neat square and remove the waste wax. Slice under each sheet and gently pull it free from the board.

3 Press the white sheet onto the red sheet and roll them up together tightly to make a Swiss roll of the two wax colors. Squeeze along the length of the roll as you go so that any trapped air is pressed out.

4 Using a sharp blade, cut one end off the cane to straighten it and then cut about ten thin slices, each about ⅛in (3mm) thick. Before the slices cool and become brittle, press them onto the surface of the candle, using a dab of wax glue to hold each in place.

5 Melt the remaining white wax and pour it onto the hot water in the dipping can. Hold the candle by its wick and dip it several times. The slices will be covered with a wax coating and the spaces between will begin to fill. With a sharp knife, pare off the wax covering the slices.

6 Dip again and the spaces between will fill further. Repeat the paring and dipping until the candle has a smooth surface. When the candle is lit, the spiral whorls will glow as they are illuminated from within.

gold leaf pyramid

Flakes of gold, silver and copper leaf decorate this exquisite candle for an opulent effect. True gold leaf costs a fortune but you can use the Dutch, or artificial, leaf instead provided that you varnish it afterwards to prevent tarnishing.

you will need

- Glue stick
- Tall cream pyramid candle
- Metallic leaf flakes of gold, silver and copper
- Damp cloth
- Candle varnish
- Brush

timing 30 minutes

tip This project uses flakes of metal leaf in a mix of colors which is available from craft suppliers. Alternatively, you can simply tear ordinary artificial leaf into small pieces to make your own flakes.

1 Smear the glue stick over the bottom third of one side of the pyramid candle. The glue will dry quickly so do not apply too much at one time.

2 Pick up a pinch of the leaf flakes and sprinkle them over the glue, patting the flakes down with your fingertip. This is a messy job because it is hard to avoid getting your finger sticky so keep a damp cloth handy to wipe your fingers from time to time.

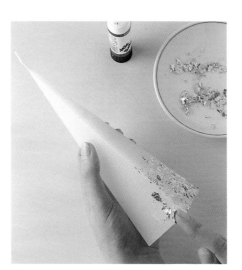

3 Apply more glue as necessary and build up the flakes so that they are thicker at the bottom of the candle and they spread out higher up. Apply glue to the second side and pat on flakes in the same way. It is easier to work on only two sides of the candle at a time and leave the remaining two sides to complete later.

4 When the glue has dried and you are happy with the result, brush a coat of candle varnish over the flakes to hold them in place and to seal them. You can varnish the areas above the leaf as well if you want the candle to be shiny all over. Repeat to apply flakes to the remaining two sides of the candle and varnish in the same way. Candle varnish does not affect the candle's burning properties.

crackle candles

Soft pastels, reminiscent of the sun-bleached colors of the Mediterranean, decorate these pretty crackle candles. I used a proprietary crackle medium that is available from art and craft stores and can be adapted for candles. It is used with ordinary acrylic paint so you can mix colors to match your room or home furnishings.

you will need

- Dark blue, white and red acrylic paint
- Saucer or palette for mixing
- Wide brush
- Dark blue molded cube or pillar candle, 2½in (6cm) diameter, made
- with a 1in (25mm) wick
- Water pot
- Soft rag
- Crackle medium for acrylic paint
- Sharp knife

timing 30 minutes plus 1 hour drying time

tip This project uses pale pink paint over a dark candle to provide the contrast for the crackle lines. Try using a pale candle and dark paint for a reversed effect.

safety note When the sides of a candle are decorated with a thick layer of paint or paper, the candle used should be made with a small wick so that the flame will burn down in a cavity about 1in (2.5cm) wide and the sides of the candle will not be spoiled, or catch fire.

1 Pour a little dark blue paint into the mixing saucer or palette and brush this lightly over the candle surface. Rub off with a soft cloth before it dries to leave a thin film of acrylic paint on the candle surface. Leave to dry.

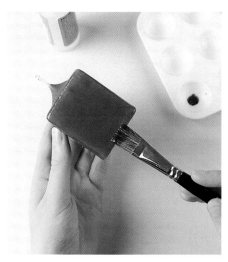

2 Paint the candle with the crackle medium, following the manufacturers' instructions. The thin film of acrylic paint will provide a key for the crackle coat which otherwise would not stick to the wax surface. Leave the crackle coat to dry for about 1 hour, or according to the instructions on the bottle.

3 Pour about 1 tablespoon of white paint into the saucer and mix in ¼ teaspoon of red paint to make a pale pastel pink. Add water if necessary to make a thin, creamy paint mixture. Paint a thick coat of this over the dried crackle medium with large, swift brush strokes.

4 The crackling will start within moments so only work on one section at a time and apply paint thickly so that it does not look streaky. Do not try to paint over the area again or the crackle effect will be spoiled.

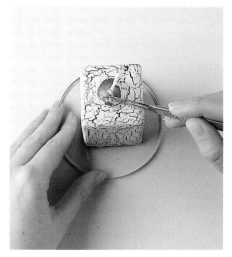

5 You will need to leave a 1in (2.5cm) diameter circle of unpainted wax around the wick or the paint will prevent the candle from burning properly. To get a neat edge, crackle the whole of the top of the candle, then cut a circle round the wick with the knife and peel off the paint.

leaf-wrapped candles

The gossamer effects of skeleton leaves lit from within by a candle flame provide

a wonderful combination of fragility and fire. The dried foliage is wrapped round

a drinking glass for safety so that the flame is kept well away from the leaves.

you will need

- 5 skeleton leaves in toning colors (cream, ochre and rust used here)
- Drinking glass, about 5in (13cm) tall and 2½in (6.5cm) diameter

- Scissors
- Craft glue
- Natural colored raffia
- Round white pillar candle, to fit inside the tumbler

timing 30 minutes

tip Skeleton leaves are available from craft suppliers and come in many beautiful colors. Alternatively, try wrapping the glass in fresh green leaves for a completely different effect.

1 Hold each leaf up against the glass and check that it is a good size. The tip of the leaf should protrude no more than 1in (2.5cm) above the rim of the glass for safety reasons. Trim the base of each leaf if necessary.

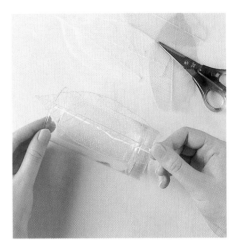

2 Squeeze a thin line of craft glue down the glass and press on the first leaf, positioning the central vein all along the line of glue.

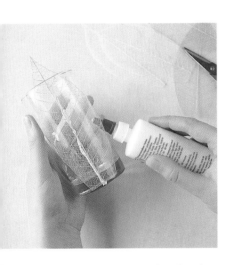

3 Tack the sides of the leaf to the glass with dabs of glue, curving the leaf around the glass. Use just enough glue to hold the leaf or it will seep through and spoil the surface.

4 Repeat with the other leaves, spacing them round the glass and gluing each central vein in place. Tack down the sides of each leaf with dabs of glue – the leaves should overlap on either side by about ½–1in (13–25mm).

5 Take several lengths of raffia and bind them round the center of the glass, holding the leaves in place. Tie a knot and then double the raffia back on itself and tie again in an attractive knot. Trim the ends of the raffia and arrange them to finish. Place the candle inside the tumbler.

outdoor candles

projects

barbecue flares

Giant candles for the outdoors, barbecue flares are fun to make and not difficult. They will burn

happily in both wind and rain for up to 3 hours, depending on their length. In this project the flares

have been decorated with drizzles of strongly dyed microcrystalline hard wax.

you will need

- A strip of cotton fabric, about 40in (1m) long and 2in (5cm) wide (old T-shirt fabric is ideal)
- Bamboo plant stake, about 4ft (120cm) long
- Masking tape
- 2in (5cm) length of wick for a 3in (75mm) thick candle (or larger), primed
- 7oz (200g) paraffin wax

- Red and orange wax dye
- Wax melting pan
- Dipping can filled with 160°F (70°C) hot water
- Thermometer
- Microcrystalline hard wax
- Small pitcher for pouring
- Roasting pan

timing 45 minutes

tip Barbecue flares burn with a strong flame so plant them firmly in the ground out of doors and keep them away from anything flammable.

1 Wrap the fabric strip round the stake until about 12in (30cm) of one end is covered. The fabric should protrude about ½in (13mm) from the end to allow easy lighting. Tape the ends down with masking tape to secure.

2 Tuck the length of wick into the fabric at the end of the stake and tape it in place. Melt some wax in a small pitcher and, holding the fabric-covered end over a pan, soak the fabric with molten wax to prime it. Melt the remaining wax and pour it on top of the hot water in the dipping can. The wax and water both need to be heated to about 160°F (70°C).

3 Dip the fabric-covered end of the stake into the wax (follow instructions for dipping on page 72) and continue dipping until the candle is about 1¼in (3cm) thick and all the fabric has been covered in wax. Add red dye to the dipping can and overdip several times to color the flare a bright red.

4 Melt some microcrystalline hard with some orange dye in a small pitcher. Hold the dipped end of the candle over the roasting pan to catch the drips and pour streams of orange wax over the candle.

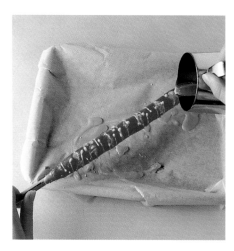

5 Twist the candle over quickly so that the wax drizzles and makes attractive trails and repeat on the other side of the flare. Leave the candle to cool overnight before lighting. Light the protruding wick – when it has burned down the flare will catch and blaze brightly.

flowerpots

Golden beeswax candles nestled into terra-cotta flowerpots create a glowing combination of warm colors, while a layer of polished pebbles holds each candle upright in its pot. Film canisters are used to make the votive candles. These little pots are ideal for outdoor use because the candle flame is sheltered from the breeze.

you will need

For four votive candles:

- Four film canisters
- Vegetable oil and brush
- 2oz (50g) paraffin wax
- 2oz (50g) beeswax
- 1 tbsp (10g) stearin
- Wax melting pan or metal pitcher
- Thermometer
- Skewer
- Four 2½in (6cm) lengths of 1in (25mm) wick, primed

- Four wick holders

For each pot:

- Dark brown, red and white acrylic paint
- Saucer for mixing
- Small sponge
- One terra-cotta flowerpot, 5in (13cm) diameter
- Polished pebbles or stones

timing Candles: 30 minutes plus setting time
Pots: 20 minutes plus drying time

tip The beeswax mixture smells delicious while it burns and makes long-lasting candles. Paraffin wax mixed with beeswax is easier to mold than pure beeswax which is very sticky.

1 Brush all over the inside of the film canisters with vegetable oil. Melt the waxes together with the stearin and when the temperature reaches 175°F (80°C), pour the wax into each canister, filling to just below the top.

2 When the surface of the wax in each canister has formed a skin, pierce the center and insert a wick, clipping it into a wick holder. Allow to partly cool and then pierce and top up the wax as usual. Leave to cool thoroughly and then remove from the molds and trim the wicks.

3 Squeeze some brown and red paint into the saucer and mix to make a dark terra-cotta. Use the sponge to brush this over the sides of the flowerpot, keeping the strokes horizontal and streaky. Allow to dry for 10 minutes.

4 Water down some white paint and sponge over the flowerpot, again using horizontal strokes and giving a streaky effect. Leave the paint to dry.

5 Place a layer of pebbles in the bottom of the pot and set one of the candles in the center. Place more pebbles around the candle, ensuring that it is firmly held upright. The candle wick should be below the rim of the pot so that it is sheltered from wind.

coconut shells

The gold leaf lining in these coconut shells reflects the candle flame with an opulent glow which
is emphasized by the rough exterior. Coconut candle scent is used to fragrance the white wax.

you will need

- Coconut
- Hacksaw
- Large bowl
- Knife
- Scouring pad
- Gold leaf size
- Paintbrush
- 5½in (14cm) square sheet of artificial gold leaf for each half coconut
- Varnish and brush
- Metal or paper core wick for a 4in (10cm) candle, primed
- Wick sustainer
- Pliers
- Wax glue
- Wick holder
- Small bowl
- 3½oz (100g) paraffin wax
- 1 tbsp (10g) microcrystalline soft (optional)
- Wax melting pan or metal pitcher
- Coconut candle scent
- Skewer

timing Cutting the coconut: 30 minutes at least. Allow overnight drying. Applying gold leaf: 30 minutes Making the candle: 30 minutes plus setting time

tip The coconut shells can be stabilized in an upright position with a ring of air drying clay as for the scallop shells on page 126. Alternatively, nestle them in a tray of sand for a desert island look!

1 Cut the coconut in half with the hacksaw, catching any milk that is inside the coconut in a bowl placed strategically below it. Coconut shells are very hard to cut so allow plenty of time to do this and be careful. Cut away the white flesh with a knife and remove it from the coconut. Scour out the coconut halves with a scouring pad to remove any loose material. Rinse with water and leave to dry overnight in a warm place.

2 Brush a generous coating of gold leaf size over the whole of the inside of one of the coconut halves. Leave to dry for 15 minutes, or according to the manufacturer's instructions. The size should be tacky but not wet when you apply the leaf.

3 Tear off pieces of leaf about 2in (5cm) long and 1in (2.5cm) wide and lay them onto the sized inside of the coconut, brushing them down with a soft brush. Overlap layers to get a complete covering and brush away the excess. There is no need to apply leaf to the very bottom of the shell which will be under the wax.

continued ▶

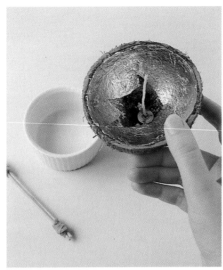

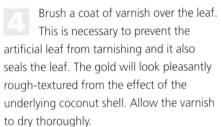

4 Brush a coat of varnish over the leaf. This is necessary to prevent the artificial leaf from tarnishing and it also seals the leaf. The gold will look pleasantly rough-textured from the effect of the underlying coconut shell. Allow the varnish to dry thoroughly.

5 Cut a length of primed metal core wick, as deep as the coconut shell plus about ⅜in (10mm). Attach one end to a wick sustainer and fix this to the bottom of the coconut shell with wax glue. Clip the other end in place with a wick holder. Stand the coconut in a small bowl to keep it upright.

6 Heat the waxes together until they have just melted. Stir ½ teaspoon of coconut candle scent into the mixture and fill the coconut to about ¾in (2cm) below the top of the shell. Leave to cool until the center has sunk around the wick.

7 Reheat the wax until it has just melted and top up the candle to just above the original layer. Leave to cool and then trim the wick to ⅜in (10mm).

jar lanterns

Lanterns are always delightful, with their bright flames shining through a small window. This project uses a recycled jam jar for the lantern, which is covered with red mulberry paper for a touch of oriental splendor. A group of lanterns hung in trees will make a glorious display.

continued ▶

you will need

- A4 sheet of scarlet mulberry paper
- Straight-sided 454g (1lb) jam jar
- Triangle
- Pencil
- Scissors
- Template (see page 140)
- Craft glue

- 39in (2m) gilt or gold colored wire, 20 gauge (or about 1mm thick)
- Hand drill
- Wire cutters
- Pliers
- Gold glass paint outliner tube with a fine tip
- Tea light

 timing 1 hour

tip Silk, or mulberry, paper comes in a wonderful selection of colors so you can make lanterns of all colors to decorate your garden. If you do not have a hand drill, twist the wire by hand: instead of clamping the ends in the drill, tie them around a stick and turn the stick to twist the wire.

safety note If you hang the lanterns in trees, keep overhanging branches well away from the flames.

1 Wrap the paper sheet lengthwise around the jar. Mark where the two sides overlap and again about 2in (5cm) above the rim. Use the triangle to draw lines across the sheet at these marks, keeping the top line at right angles to the side. Cut out the resulting rectangle.

2 Fold the paper in half lengthwise to find the center and trace the template of the lantern window onto it. Cut out the window.

3 Spread craft glue over the sides of the jam jar, avoiding the area where you will place the window. Press the paper onto the glue, smoothing it down all round the jar and butting together the edges where they meet at the back.

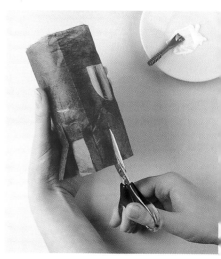

4 Make vertical cuts in the paper all round the top of the jar and press the resulting flaps down onto the jar top, overlapping them to make a neat fit. Trim along the top edge of the jar so that no paper overhangs into the jar.

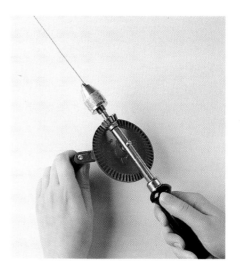

5 Now cut vertical lines in the paper all around the base of the jar, in the same way. Press the flaps around the bottom of the jar, overlapping as before. Cut out a circle of paper, the same size as the jar bottom, and glue it in place.

6 While the paper is drying, cut three lengths of wire, each 24in (60cm) long. Fold one length in half and slip it round a table leg or other strong support. Clamp the two ends of the wire into the chuck of the drill.

7 Holding the wire taut, wind the drill and the wire will begin to twist. As you continue to wind, the wire will twist evenly all along its length and any kinks will disappear. When the whole length of wire is twisted, cut it off where it is joined to the support. Repeat to make two more twisted lengths.

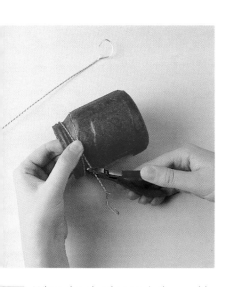

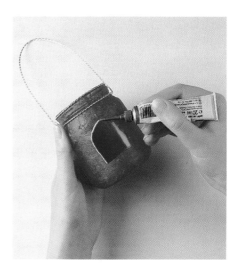

8 When the glued paper is thoroughly dry, wrap one length of twisted wire round the neck of the jar and trim it so that you have about 1in (2.5cm) extra at each end to twist together. Remove it from the jar to attach the handle.

9 Form the second length of wire into a gentle curve for the handle and make a hook at each end. Thread the first wire through these hooks and wrap it around the jar neck, twisting its ends to secure at the back and pressing them down so there are no sharp edges. Twist the third piece of wire around the top edge of the jar for extra decoration.

10 Space the handle hooks evenly so that they are on opposite sides of the jar and the lantern hangs straight. Take care that you do not tear the glued paper. Finally outline the window along the paper edge with gold outliner. Place a tea light in the lantern and hang it up to display.

scallop shells

Scallop shells make delightful container candles. Their large size means that you can use a relatively large wick, which produces a big bright flame that will burn for about two hours. They look enchanting lining a garden path on a still night.

you will need

For each candle:

- Small piece of air drying clay (a ball about ¾in (20mm) in diameter)
- Tile or plate
- A large scallop shell, approximately 5in (13cm) across the shell
- 3½oz (100g) paraffin wax
- 1 tbsp (10g) microcrystalline soft wax (optional)

- Orange wax dye
- Wax melting pan or metal pitcher
- Thermometer
- Skewer
- Wick for a 2½in (65mm) candle, 2¼in (6cm) long, primed
- Wick holder
- Super glue

 **timing** 30 minutes plus setting time and overnight for the clay to dry

tip You do not need to make a support for the shell if you are going to place it on gravel or grass. If you cannot get scallop shells, any large flat shells such as oyster shells can be used instead.

1 To make a support for the shell, form the air drying clay into a crescent shape and press this onto a tile. With the shell held level, press it onto the clay, positioning it so that the crescent cups the shell and holds it level.

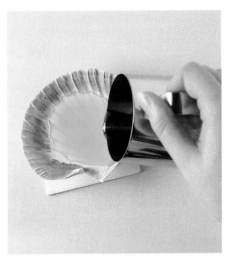

2 Melt the waxes together with enough dye to make a pale orange. Heat to 175°F (80°C) and pour the wax into the shell, filling it to within ³⁄₁₆in (5mm) of the lowest point of the top edge.

3 Leave the wax to set until it has formed a skin over the top about ⅛in (3 mm) thick. Pierce through the center of the skin with a skewer and push in the primed wick. Clip the wick in a wick holder and leave to cool again.

4 When the wax has set and the center has sunk but it is still warm, top off with more 175°F (80°C) wax to just above the first pour. There is no need to pierce around the wick when using such a shallow container.

5 When the wax is cool, remove the wick holder and trim the wick to ½in (13mm). Leave the shell on the tile for 24 hours until the clay has dried. Finally, squeeze some super glue between the hard clay and shell to attach the support firmly to the shell.

floating citronella candles

These big floating candles are scented with citronella and, when burnt, their large flames give off a delicious lemony scent which helps to keep away the biters and buzzers that can trouble your barbecue. Float them in a garden urn with water lilies for a fairy-tale scene.

you will need

For five floating candles:

- Standard muffin pan with cavities approximately 2½in (6cm) diameter and at least ¾in (2cm) deep
- Vegetable oil and brush
- 5½oz (150g) paraffin wax

- 1 tbsp (10g) stearin
- Yellow wax dye
- Wax melting pan or metal pitcher
- Thermometer
- Citronella essential oil
- Five 2in (5cm) lengths of 2½in (65mm) wick, primed
- Several skewers

timing 30 minutes plus setting time

tip These candles should burn for at least one hour. If you use a muffin pan with deeper cavities, you can make candles that will last longer. Make sure that you insert the wicks in the center of each candle or they will not burn evenly.

1 Brush five of the muffin pan cavities with a thin coating of oil. Melt the wax with the stearin and dye to give a bright yellow color.

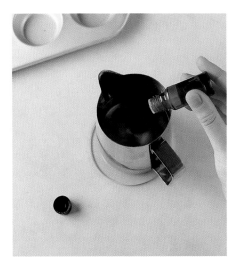

2 When the wax temperature reaches 175°F (80°C), remove the pan from the heat and add 15 drops of citronella oil and stir it into the wax. Adding the oil just before pouring helps to retain the aroma, which will evaporate if heated for too long.

3 Pour the wax mixture into the oiled cavities, filling them to just below the top. Leave them to cool until a ⅛in (3mm) skin has formed over the surface.

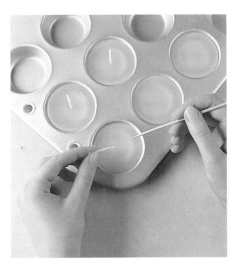

4 Pierce into the center of each candle with a skewer and insert a primed wick. Leave to cool again for about 15 minutes by which time the surface will have sunk and the wicks set into the wax. Top off with more hot wax, filling the sunken center. The hot wax will spread out to make a neat circle around the wick. Do not overfill or the fresh wax will overflow the edges of the candle.

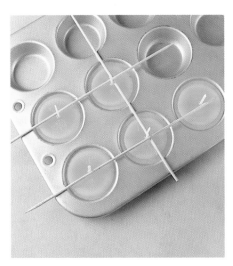

5 The hot wax will cause the wicks to sag, so prop them upright with several skewers and leave to cool thoroughly. Finally, remove the candles from the molds and trim the wicks.

paper lanterns

Simple ideas are often the most striking and these paper bag votives are made from a single sheet of paper. The apparently intricate windows are snipped into a folded section of the paper before assembling the bag. They look magical positioned along a pathway or drive – the bags glow when the candles inside them are lit.

you will need

- Template (see page 141)
- A4 sheet of plain white paper
- Pencil
- Small sharp scissors
- Soft eraser
- Craft glue
- Tea light
- Glass jar

timing 10–15 minutes per bag

tip Once you have mastered the technique, you will find it easy to invent cut-out patterns for yourself. Try using colored paper for the bags, or colored paper lined with a sheet of white paper for maximum glow.

safety note Never put an unprotected candle inside a paper bag. Stand the candle in a glass jar and place this into the bag.

1 Enlarge the template on page 141 on a photo-copier and trace it lightly onto a plain sheet of paper in pencil. Fold the sheet along the horizontal line of the central cross and along the vertical line. Only crease along the lines of the cross – do not continue to the edges of the paper.

2 Hold the folded paper with the pencilled design facing out. Snip out the main areas of the design first, then snip away the small wedges. Be careful not to cut away any of the white areas, or parts of the design may come away.

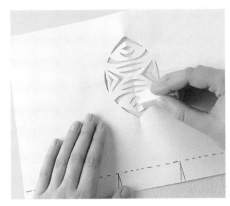

3 Open out the folded paper and the design will be revealed. Smooth down the folds and carefully erase all the pencil lines or they will show when the paper bag is lit up.

4 Fold along the fold line at the bottom of the sheet and clip out the notches to make the flaps for the bottom of the bag.

5 Apply a line of glue along the vertical flap. Curve the sheet into a cylinder and press the flap onto the opposite edge of the sheet, holding until it is stuck firmly. Push the flaps into place to form the base of the bag and glue to secure.

6 Cut a piece of paper the same size as the base of the bag and glue it over the flaps. Light a tea light and place it into a glass jar or tumbler. Carefully slide this into the bag by letting the glass slip down slowly.

gallery

calming and natural

Soft grays and stone colors have a soothing quality and all these candles help create an atmosphere of tranquillity and peace. The colors and textures combined with the shells and pebbles are reminiscent of a Japanese garden with combed sand, rough-hewn granite and water features.

1. This marvelous cubed candle has the effect of a block of rough granite. It is displayed in a simple frosted glass holder that provides a perfect contrast.

2. A gel candle tinted lightly with a periwinkle blue dye contains suspended shells and a scattering of bubbles for a truly watery effect.

3. A soft gray crackled candle is displayed in an oriental-style holder.

4. Myriad tiny shells are included in the cool blue wax of this large pillar candle. The shells are clearly visible through the wax and will be lit from within as the candle burns down.

5. Overdipping with microcrystalline hard wax has given this pearly beige candle a beautifully random surface effect.

6. Pebble candles in soft, natural colors can be made with latex molds. Pouring the wax when it has slightly cooled gives a mottled surface.

7. This lovely candle looks rather like a prehistoric pot with its bold surface striations and earthy shape. You can create a similar effect by texturing the surface of a black candle with a fork and rubbing white acrylic paint into the grooves.

gallery

cool and chic

Sophisticated shapes and subtle colors give this group of candles a tasteful elegance. Candleholders are also extremely important in the art of displaying candles and those shown here demonstrate how a simple candle in the right container can become a work of art!

1. A cream church pillar candle is displayed in a plain glass hurricane candleholder for a simple statement that has universal appeal.

2. This heavy glass container looks superb when lit from within by a single votive candle.

3. Smooth gray wax is used for this sophisticated molded candle to enhance the architectural effect.

4. & 5. These large molded candles combine bold geometric shapes with a faux weathered surface and earthy colors.

6. Black and white always create an elegant color scheme and here they are used for a two-tone candle with slight surface texturing to add interest.

7. Worked silver encases a deep turquoise glass votive holder for a touch of oriental splendor.

8. A smooth lilac egg candle demonstrates how effective pure simplicity can be.

9. Beaded votive holders are increasingly popular and this pretty design combines pearl beads and netting for a delicate effect.

10. This delightful group displays six small cube candles in a white ceramic holder. The spaces between the candles form an important part of the design.

gallery

vivid color and texture

Singing colors combined with strong, bold shapes and exotic textures produce an exciting group of candles. You can group candles of contrasting primary colors to produce a carnival effect, or use a single strong color for a potent accent on a dinner table.

1. This blue and white pillar candle displays marvelous swirls and shapes that are reminiscent of an underwater ice cave.

2. A smooth molded egg candle displays a tilted layer of deep blue.

3. Indented circles texture the surface of this bold crimson pillar candle. This type of candle can be first sculpted in clay to make a latex mold.

4. Deep blue ball candles display a pleasing rough surface that is achieved by pouring partly cooled wax into the molds.

5. The textured sides of these cube candles contrast well with their shiny rounded edges for a popular 'worn' effect.

6. This massive molded orange multiwick candle has a rough surface and the result is reminiscent of a large cheese!

7. Consecutive graded wax layers make up this molded pillar candle. Each new layer is poured when the previous one is cool so that the colors do not merge.

8. Molded hexagonal candles with sharply defined edges and a slight surface texture give a strong, stylish impression.

9. These simple textured glass containers filled with brightly colored wax would be perfect displayed as an accent color on a dressing table.

10. Overdipping tapers in bright colors gives added interest to their traditional shape.

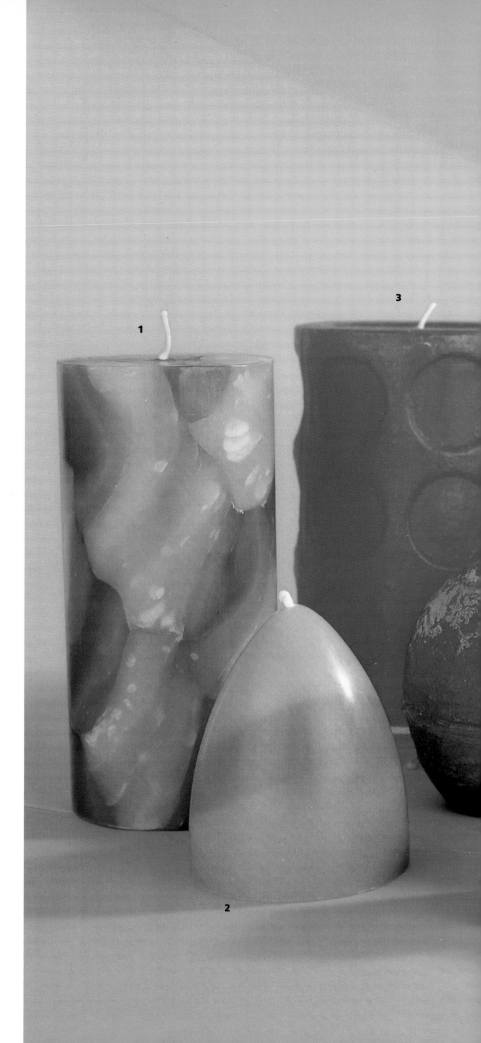

templates

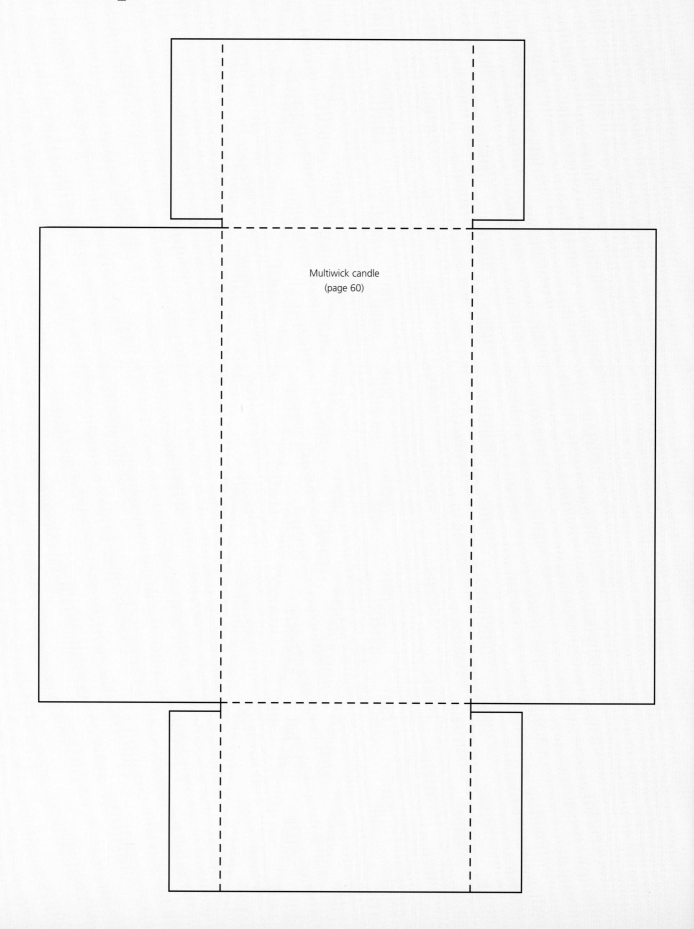

Multiwick candle
(page 60)

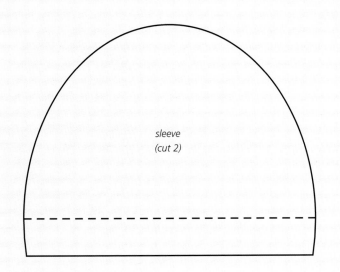

sleeve
(cut 2)

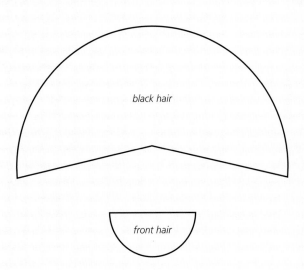

black hair

front hair

Little angel
(page 84)

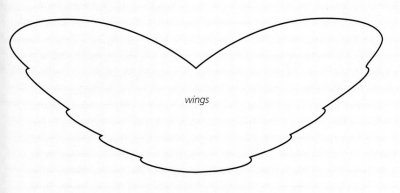

wings

face

hands
(cut 2)

'Cave art'
(page 92)

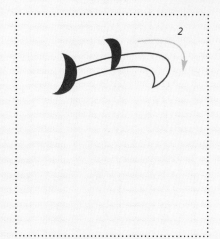

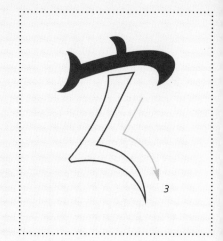

Chinese calligraphy (page 98)

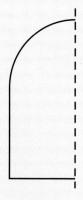

Incised ferns
(page 104)

Jar lantern
(page 123)

Paper lanterns
(page 130)

*To enlarge this template onto A4 paper,
precisely place the bottom right-hand corner of
this page into the 'zero' corner of a
photocopier's glass platen and set the zoom to
141% (sometimes called the A4 to A3 setting).*

*fold
line*

suppliers

USA

Bitter Creek Candle Supply, Inc.
Route 4, Box 184
Ashland, WI 54806
Tel: (715) 278-3900
www.candlesupply.com

Candles and More
Bobby's Craft Boutique Inc.
120 Hillside Avenue
Williston Park, New York 11596
Tel: 516 877 2499
Email: candles@craftcave.com
www.craftcave.com

Candles and Supplies
301 South 3rd Street (Rt. 309)
Coopersburg, PA 18036
Tel: 610 282 5522
www.candlesandsupplies.com

General Wax & Candle Co.
6863 Beck Avenue
North Hollywood, CA 91605
Tel: 800 929 7867
Fax: 818 764 3878

GloryBee Foods Inc.
PO Box 2744
Eugene, OR 97402
Tel: 800 456 7923
www.glorybee.com
suppliers of beeswax

Hanna's Candle Co.
2700 South Armstrong Ave.
Fayetteville, AR 72701
Tel: 800 327 9826
www.hannascandles.com

Kewl Candle Factory
1829 Kingshighway
St. Louis, MO 63110
Tel: 314 477 5258
www.gelcandlesupply.com
suppliers of jelly wax

Missy's Candles
366 US Route 35
Ray, OH 45672
Tel: 888 647 7971
www.candlemaking.com

Pourette Manufacturing
1418 NW 53rd Street
PO Box 70469
Seattle, WA 98107
Tel: 800 888 WICK
Fax: 206 789 3640

WAAGE
PO Box 337
Kenilworth, NJ 07033
Tel: 908 245 9363
www.waage.com

The Wax House
Scent Masters
15009 Held Circle
Cold Spring, MN 56320
Tel: (320) 363 0411
www.waxhouse.com

Yankee Candle Company
PO Box 110
South Deerfield, MA 01373
Tel: 800 243 1776
Fax: 413 665 8321

Canada

Ashburnham Crafting Supplies
120 Hunter Street East
Peterborough
Ontario K9H 1G6
Tel: 705 742 6083
www.sympatico.ca

Lynden House International Inc.
5527-137 Avenue, Edmonton
Alberta T5L 3L4
Tel: 780 448 1994
Fax: 780 448 0086
www.lyndenhouse.net

United Kingdom

Candle Makers Suppliers
28 Blythe Road
London W14 0HA
Tel: 020 7602 4031/2
Fax: 020 7602 2796
Email: candles@candlemakers.co.uk
www.candlemakers.co.uk

The Candle Shop
30 The Market
Covent Garden
London WC2E 8RE
Tel: 020 7836 9815
Fax: 020 7240 8065
Email: cgcc@candles-sales.com
www.candlesontheweb.co.uk

Caesar Ceramics
358 Edgware Road
London W2 1EB
Tel: 020 7224 9671
Fax: 020 7224 9854
Email: sales@caesarceramics.co.uk
www.caesarceramics.co.uk

Homecrafts Direct
Unit 2, Wanlip Road
Syston, Leicester
Leicestershire LE7 1PA
Tel: 0116 269 7733
Email: info@homecrafts.co.uk
www.homecrafts.co.uk

Panduro Hobby
Westway House,
Transport Avenue, Brentford
Middlesex TW8 9HF
Tel: 020 8847 6161
Fax: 020 8847 5073
www.panduro.co.uk

Senses Candle Design
5G Atlas Business Centre
Oxgate Lane, Staples Corner
London NW2 7HJ
Tel/Fax: 020 8450 3255